Agnes Repplier

**Points of View**

Agnes Repplier

**Points of View**

ISBN/EAN: 9783337298456

Printed in Europe, USA, Canada, Australia, Japan

Cover: Foto ©Thomas Meinert / pixelio.de

More available books at **www.hansebooks.com**

# POINTS OF VIEW

BY

AGNES REPPLIER, LITT. D.

BOSTON AND NEW YORK
HOUGHTON MIFFLIN COMPANY
The Riverside Press Cambridge

# CONTENTS.

PAGE

A PLEA FOR HUMOR . . . . . . . . 1
ENGLISH LOVE-SONGS . . . . . . . 30
BOOKS THAT HAVE HINDERED ME . . . . 64
LITERARY SHIBBOLETHS . . . . . . 78
FICTION IN THE PULPIT . . . . . . . 105
PLEASURE: A HERESY . . . . . . . 136
ESOTERIC ECONOMY . . . . . . . . 166
SCANDERBEG . . . . . . . . . 189
ENGLISH RAILWAY FICTION . . . . . . 209

" Scanderbeg " is reprinted from " The Catholic World "
by permission of the publishers.

# POINTS OF VIEW.

## A PLEA FOR HUMOR.

MORE than half a dozen years have passed since Mr. Andrew Lang, startled for once out of his customary light-heartedness, asked himself, and his readers, and the ghost of Charles Dickens — all three powerless to answer — whether the dismal seriousness of the present day was going to last forever; or whether, when the great wave of earnestness had rippled over our heads, we would pluck up heart to be merry and, if needs be, foolish once again. Not that mirth and folly are in any degree synonymous, as of old; for the merry fool, too scarce, alas, even in the times when Jacke of Dover hunted for him in the highways, has since then grown to be rarer than a phœnix. He has carried his cap and bells, and jests and laughter, elsewhere, and has left us to the

mercies of the serious fool, who is by no
means so seductive a companion. If the Cocque-
cigrües are in possession of the land, and if
they are tenants exceedingly hard to evict,
it is because of the connivance and encouragement they receive from those to whom we innocently turn for help: from the poets, and
novelists, and men of letters, whose plain duty
it is to brighten and make glad our days.

"It is obvious," sighs Mr. Birrell deject-
edly, "that many people appear to like a
drab-colored world, hung around with dusky
shreds of philosophy;" but it is more obvious
still that, whether they like it or not, the
drapings grow a trifle dingier every year, and
that no one seems to have the courage to tack
up something gay. What is much worse,
even those bits of wanton color which have
rested generations of weary eyes are being
rapidly obscured by sombre and intricate
scroll-work, warranted to oppress and fatigue.
The great masterpieces of humor, which have
kept men young by laughter, are being tried
in the courts of an orthodox morality, and
found lamentably wanting; or else, by way of
giving them another chance, they are being

subjected to the *peine forte et dure* of modern analysis, and are revealing hideous and melancholy meanings in the process. I have always believed that Hudibras owes its chilly treatment at the hands of critics — with the single and most genial exception of Sainte-Beuve — to the absolute impossibility of twisting it into something serious. Strive as we may, we cannot put a new construction on those vigorous old jokes, and to be simply and barefacedly amusing is no longer considere a sufficient *raison d'être.* It is the most significant token of our ever-increasing " sense of moral responsibility in literature " that we should be always trying to graft our own conscientious purposes upon those authors who, happily for themselves, lived and died before virtue, colliding desperately with cakes and ale, had imposed such depressing obligations.

" Don Quixote," says Mr. Shorthouse with unctuous gravity, " will come in time to be recognized as one of the saddest books ever written ; " and, if the critics keep on expounding it much longer, I truly fear it will. It may be urged that Cervantes himself was low enough to think it exceedingly funny; but

then one advantage of our new and keener
insight into literature is to prove to us how
indifferently great authors understood their
own masterpieces.  Shakespeare, we are told,
knew comparatively little about Hamlet, and
he is to be congratulated on his limitations.
Defoe would hardly recognize Robinson Crusoe
as "a picture of civilization," having innocently supposed it to be quite the reverse;
and he would be as amazed as we are to learn
from Mr. Frederic Harrison that his book
contains "more psychology, more political
economy, and more anthropology than are to
be found in many elaborate treatises on these
especial subjects," — blighting words which
I would not even venture to quote if I thought
that any boy would chance to read them, and
so have one of the pleasures of his young life
destroyed.  As for Don Quixote, which its
author persisted in regarding with such mis-
placed levity, it has passed through many bewildering vicissitudes.  It has figured bravely
as a satire on the Duke of Lerma, on Charles
V., on Philip II., on Ignatius Loyola, — Cervantes was the most devout of Catholics, —
and on the Inquisition, which, fortunately, did

not think so. In fact, there is little or nothing which it has not meant in its time; and
now, having attained that deep spiritual in-
wardness which we have been recently told is
lacking in poor Goldsmith, we are requested
by Mr. Shorthouse to refrain from all brutal
laughter, but, with a shadowy smile and a
profound seriousness, to attune ourselves to
the proper state of receptivity. Old-fashioned,
coarse-minded people may perhaps ask, " But
if we are not to laugh at Don Quixote, at
whom are we, please, to laugh?" — a question which I, for one, would hardly dare to
answer. Only, after reading the following
curious sentence, extracted from a lately published volume of criticism, I confess to finding
myself in a state of mental perplexity, utterly
alien to mirth. " How much happier," its
author sternly reminds us, " was poor Don
Quixote in his energetic career, in his earnest
redress of wrong, and in his ultimate triumph
over self, than he could have been in the gnaw-
ing reproach and spiritual stigma which a
yielding to weakness never failingly entails!"
Beyond this point it would be hard to go.
Were these things really spoken of the "in-

genious gentleman " of La Mancha, or of
John Howard, or George Peabody, or perhaps Elizabeth Fry, — or is there no longer
such a thing as a recognized absurdity in the
world ?

Another gloomy indication of the departure
of humor from our midst is the tendency of
philosophical writers to prove by analysis that,
if they are not familiar with the thing itself,
they at least know of what it should consist.
Mr. Shorthouse's depressing views about Don
Quixote are merely introduced as illustrating
a very scholarly and comfortless paper on the
subtle qualities of mirth. No one could deal
more gracefully and less humorously with his
topic than does Mr. Shorthouse, and we are
compelled to pause every now and then and
reassure ourselves as to the subject matter of
his eloquence. Professor Everett has more
recently and more cheerfully defined for us
the Philosophy of the Comic, in a way which,
if it does not add to our gayety, cannot be accused of plunging us deliberately into gloom.
He thinks, indeed, — and small wonder, — that
there is " a genuine difficulty in distinguishing between the comic and the tragic," and

that what we need is some formula which shall accurately interpret the precise qualities of each; and he is disposed to illustrate his theory by dwelling on the tragic side of Falstaff, which is, of all injuries, the grimmest and hardest to forgive. Falstaff is now the forlorn hope of those who love to laugh, and when he is taken away from us, as soon, alas! he will be, and sleeps with Don Quixote in the "dull cold marble" of an orthodox sobriety, how shall we make merry our souls? Mr. George Radford, who enriched the first volume of "Obiter Dicta" with such a loving study of the fat-witted old knight, tells us reassuringly that by laughter man is distinguished from the beasts, though the cares and sorrows of life have all but deprived him of this elevating grace, and degraded him into a brutal solemnity. Then comes along a rare genius like Falstaff, who restores the power of laughter, and transforms the stolid brute once more into a man, and who accordingly has the highest claim to our grateful and affectionate regard. That there are those who persist in looking upon him as a selfish and worthless fellow is, from Mr. Radford's point of view, a sorrowful instance

of human thanklessness and perversity. But
this I take to be the enamored and exagger-
ated language of a too faithful partisan. Mor-
ally speaking, Falstaff has not a leg to stand
upon, and there *is* a tragic element lurking
always amid the fun. But, seen in the broad
sunlight of his transcendent humor, this
shadow is as the half-pennyworth of bread to
his own noble ocean of sack, and why should
we be forever trying to force it into prominence? When Charlotte Brontë advised her
friend, Ellen Nussey, to read none of Shakespeare's comedies, she was not beguiled for a
moment into regarding them as serious and
melancholy lessons of life; but with uncom-
promising directness put them down as mere
improper plays, the amusing qualities of which
were insufficient to excuse their coarseness,
and which were manifestly unfit for the "gentle Ellen's" eyes.

In fact, humor would at all times have been
the poorest excuse to offer to Miss Brontë
for any form of moral dereliction, for it was
the one quality she lacked herself, and failed
to tolerate in others. Sam Weller was apparently as obnoxious to her as was Fal-

staff, for she would not even consent to meet
Dickens, when she was being lionized in London society, — a degree of abstemiousness
on her part which it is disheartening to contemplate. It does not seem too much to say
that every shortcoming in Charlotte Brontë's
admirable work, every limitation of her splendid genius, arose primarily from her want
of humor. Her severities of judgment —
and who more severe than she? — were due
to the same melancholy cause ; for humor
is the kindliest thing alive. Compare the
harshness with which she handles her hap-
less curates, and the comparative crudity of
her treatment, with the surpassing lightness
of Miss Austen's touch as she rounds and
completes her immortal clerical portraits.
Miss Brontë tells us, in one of her letters, that
she regarded *all* curates as " highly uninteresting, narrow, and unattractive specimens of
the coarser sex," just as she found *all* the
Belgian school-girls " cold, selfish, animal, and
inferior." But to Miss Austen's keen and
friendly eye the narrowest of clergymen was
not wholly uninteresting, the most inferior of
school-girls not without some claim to our con-

sideration; even the coarseness of the male
sex was far from vexing her maidenly serenity, probably because she was unacquainted
with the Rochester type. Mr. Elton is cer-
tainly narrow, Mary Bennet extremely inferior; but their authoress only laughs at them
softly, with a quiet tolerance, and a good-
natured sense of amusement at their follies.
It was little wonder that Charlotte Brontë,
who had at all times the courage of her convictions, could not, and would not, read Jane
Austen's novels. "They have not got story
enough for me," she boldly affirmed. " I
don't want my blood curdled, but I like to
have it stirred. Miss Austen strikes me as
milk-and-watery, and, to say truth, as dull."
Of course she did! How was a woman, whose
ideas of after-dinner conversation are embod-
ied in the amazing language of Baroness Ingram and her titled friends, to appreciate the
delicious, sleepy small talk, in "Sense and Sen-
sibility," about the respective heights of the respective grandchildren? It is to Miss Brontë's
abiding lack of humor that we owe such
stately caricatures as Blanche Ingram, and all
the high-born, ill-bred company who gather

in Thornfield Hall, like a group fresh from
Madame Tussaud's ingenious workshop, and
against whose waxen unreality Jane Eyre and
Rochester, alive to their very finger-tips, contrast like twin sparks of fire. It was her lack
of humor, too, which beguiled her into as-
serting that the forty "wicked, sophistical,
and immoral French novels," which found
their way down to lonely Haworth, gave her
"a thorough idea of France and Paris," — alas,
poor misjudged France! — and which made
her think Thackeray very nearly as wicked,
sophistical, and immoral as the French novels.
Even her dislike for children was probably
due to the same irremediable misfortune; for
the humors of children are the only redeeming points amid their general naughtiness, and
vexing misbehavior. Mr. Swinburne, guiltless himself of any jocose tendencies, has made
the unique discovery that Charlotte Brontë
strongly resembles Cervantes, and that Paul
Emanuel is a modern counterpart of Don
Quixote; and well it is for our poet that the
irascible little professor never heard him hint
at such a similarity. Surely, to use one of
Mr. Swinburne's own incomparable expres-

sions, the parallel is no better than a "sub-simious absurdity."

On the other hand, we are told that Miss Austen owed her lively sense of humor to her habit of dissociating the follies of mankind from any rigid standard of right and wrong, which means, I suppose, that she never dreamed she had a mission. Nowadays, indeed, no writer is without one. We cannot even read a paper upon gypsies, and not become aware that its author is deeply imbued with a sense of his personal responsibility for these agreeable rascals, whom he insists upon our taking seriously, — as if we wanted to have anything to do with them on such terms ! "Since the time of Carlyle," says Mr. Bagehot, " earnestness has been a favorite virtue in literature ; " but Carlyle, though sharing largely in that profound melancholy which he declared to be the basis of every English soul, and though he was unfortunate enough to think Pickwick sad trash, had nevertheless a grim and eloquent humor of his own. With him, at least, earnestness never degenerated into dullness ; and while dullness may be, as he unhesitatingly affirmed, the

first requisite for a great and free people, yet
a too heavy percentage of this valuable quality
is fatal to the sprightly grace of literature.
" In our times," said an old Scotchwoman,
" there 's fully mony modern principles," and
the first of these seems to be the substitution
of a serious and critical discernment for the
light-hearted sympathy of former days. Our
grandfathers cried a little and laughed a good
deal over their books, without the smallest
sense of anxiety or responsibility in the matter ; but we are called on repeatedly to face
problems which we would rather let alone, to
dive dismally into motives, to trace subtle connections, to analyze uncomfortable sensations,
and to exercise in all cases a discreet and conscientious severity, when what we really want
and need is half an hour's amusement. There
is no stronger proof of the great change that
has swept over mankind than the sight of a
nation which used to chuckle over " Tom
Jones " absorbing a few years ago countless
editions of " Robert Elsmere." What is droller
still is that the people who read " Robert Elsmere " would think it wrong to enjoy " Tom
Jones," and that the people who enjoyed " Tom

Jones" would have thought it wrong to read
"Robert Elsmere;" and that the people who,
wishing to be on the safe side of virtue, think
it wrong to read either, are scorned greatly as
lacking true moral discrimination.

Now he would be a brave man who would
undertake to defend the utterly indefensible
literature of the past. Where it was most
humorous it was also most coarse, wanton, and
cruel; but, in banishing these objectionable
qualities, we have effectually contrived to rid
ourselves of the humor as well, and with it we
have lost one of the safest instincts of our
souls. Any book which serves to lower the
sum of human gayety is a moral delinquent;
and instead of coddling it into universal notice, and growing owlish in its gloom, we
should put it briskly aside in favor of brighter
and pleasanter things. When Father Faber
said that there was no greater help to a religious life than a keen sense of the ridiculous,
he startled a number of pious people, yet what
a luminous and cordial message it was to help
us on our way! Mr. Birrell has recorded the
extraordinary delight with which he came
across some after-dinner sally of the Rev.

Henry Martyn's; for the very thought of that ardent and fiery spirit relaxing into pleasant-ries over the nuts and wine made him appear like an actual fellow-being of our own. It is with the same feeling intensified, as I have already noted, that we read some of the letters of the early fathers, — those grave and hal-lowed figures seen through a mist of centuries, — and find them jesting at one another in the gayest and least sacerdotal manner imaginable. " Who could tell a story with more wit, who could joke so pleasantly? " sighs St. Gregory of Nazienzen of his friend St. Basil, remember-ing doubtless with a heavy heart the shafts of good-humored raillery that had brightened their lifelong intercourse. With what kindly and loving zest does Gregory, himself the most austere of men, mock at Basil's asceticism, — at those " sad and hungry banquets " of which he was invited to partake, those " ungarden-like gardens, void of pot-herbs," in which he was expected to dig! With what delightful alacrity does Basil vindicate his reputation for numor by making a most excellent joke in court, for the benefit of a brutal magistrate who fiercely threatened to tear out his liver!

"Your intention is a benevolent one," said the saint, who had been for years a confirmed invalid. "Where it is now located, it has given me nothing but trouble." Surely, as we read such an anecdote as this, we share in the curious sensation experienced by little Tom Tulliver, when, by dint of Maggie's repeated questions, he began slowly to understand that the Romans had once been real men, who were happy enough to speak their own language without any previous introduction to the Eton grammar. In like manner, when we come to realize that the fathers of the primitive Church enjoyed their quips and cranks and jests as much as do Mr. Trollope's jolly deans or vicars, we feel we have at last grasped the secret of their identity, and we appreciate the force of Father Faber's appeal to the frank spirit of a wholesome mirth.

Perhaps one reason for the scanty tolerance that humor receives at the hands of the disaffected is because of the rather selfish way in which the initiated enjoy their fun; for there is always a secret irritation about a laugh in which we cannot join. Mr. George Saintsbury is plainly of this way of thinking, and,

being blessed beyond his fellows with a love
for all that is jovial, he speaks from out of the
richness of his experience. "Those who have
a sense of humor," he says, "instead of being
quietly and humbly thankful, are perhaps a
little too apt to celebrate their joy in the face
of the afflicted ones who have it not; and the
afflicted ones only follow a general law in protesting that it is a very worthless thing, if not
a complete humbug." This spirit of exclu-
siveness on the one side and of irascibility on
the other may be greatly deplored, but who is
there among us, I wonder, wholly innocent of
blame? Mr. Saintsbury himself confesses to
a silent chuckle of delight when he thinks of
the dimly veiled censoriousness with which
Peacock's inimitable humor has been received
by one half of the reading world. In other
words, his enjoyment of the Rev. Drs. Folliott and Opimian is sensibly increased by the
reflection that a great many worthy people,
even among his own acquaintances, are, by
some mysterious law of their being, debarred
from any share in his pleasure. Yet surely
we need not be so niggardly in this matter.
There is wit enough in those two reverend

gentlemen to go all around the living earth,
and leave plenty for generations now unborn.
Each might say with Juliet, —

> " The more I give to thee,
> The more I have ; "

for wit is as infinite as love, and a deal more
lasting in its qualities.  When Peacock describes a country gentleman's range of ideas
as "nearly commensurate with that of .the
great king Nebuchadnezzar when he was
turned out to grass," he affords us a happy
illustration of the eternal fitness of humor,
for there can hardly come a time when such
an apt comparison will fail to point its meaning.

Mr. Birrell is quite as selfish in his felicity
as Mr. Saintsbury, and perfectly frank in ac·
knowledging it.  He dwells rapturously over
certain well-loved pages of "Pride and Preju-
dice," and "Mansfield Park," and then deliberately adds, "When an admirer of Miss
Austen reads these familiar passages, the smile
of satisfaction, betraying the deep inward peace
they never fail to beget, widens, like 'a circle
in the water,' as he remembers (and he is always careful to remember) how his dearest

friend, who has been so successful in life, can
no more read Miss Austen than he can read
the Moabitish Stone." The same peculiarity
is noticeable in the more ardent lovers of
Charles Lamb. They seem to want him all
to themselves, look askance upon any fellow-
being who ventures to assert a modest preference for their idol, and brighten visibly when
some ponderous critic declares the Letters to
be sad stuff, and not worth half the exasperating nonsense talked about them. Yet Lamb
flung his good things to the winds with characteristic prodigality, little recking by whom or
in what spirit they were received. How many
witticisms, I wonder, were roared into the deaf
ears of old Thomas Westwood, who heard
them not, alas, but who laughed all the same,
out of pure sociability, and with a pleasant
sense that something funny had been said!
And what of that ill-fated pun which Lamb,
in a moment of deplorable abstraction, let fall
at a funeral, to the surprise and consternation
of the mourners? Surely a man who could
joke at a funeral never meant his pleasantries
to be hoarded up for the benefit of an initiated
few, but would gladly see them the property

of all living men; ay, and of all dead men,
too, were such a distribution possible. " Damn
the age! I will write for antiquity!" he ex-
claimed, with not unnatural heat, when the
" Gypsy's Malison " was rejected by the ingenious editors of the "Gem," on the ground
that it would " shock all mothers ; " and even
this expression, uttered with pardonable irritation, manifests no solicitude for a narrow and
esoteric audience.

" Wit is useful for everything, but sufficient
for nothing," says Amiel, who probably felt
he needed some excuse for burying so much
of his Gallic sprightliness in Teutonic gloom ;
and dullness, it must be admitted, has the
distinct advantage of being useful for everybody, and sufficient for nearly everybody as
well. Nothing, we are told, is more rational
than *ennui ;* and Mr. Bagehot, contemplating
the "grave files of speechless men " who have
always represented the English land, exults
more openly and energetically even than Carlyle in the saving dullness, the superb impene-
trability, which stamps the Englishman, as it
stamped the Roman, with the sign-manual of
patient strength. Stupidity, he reminds us,

is not folly, and moreover it often insures a valuable consistency. "'What I says is this here, as I was a-saying yesterday,' is the average Englishman's notion of historical eloquence and habitual discretion." But Mr. Bagehot could well afford to trifle thus coyly with dullness, because he knew it only theoretically and as a dispassionate observer. His own roof-tree is free from the blighting presence; his own pages are guiltless of the leaden touch. It has been well said that an ordinary mortal might live for a twelvemonth like a gentleman on Hazlitt's ideas; but he might, if he were clever, shine all his life long with the reflected splendor of Mr. Bagehot's wit, and be thought to give forth a very respectable illumination. There is a telling quality in every stroke; a pitiless dexterity that drives the weapon, like a fairy's arrow, straight to some vital point. When we read that "of all pursuits ever invented by man for separating the faculty of argument from the capacity of belief, the art of debating is probably the most effective," we feel that an unwelcome statement has been expressed with Mephistophelian coolness; and remembering that these

words were uttered before Mr. Gladstone had
attained his parliamentary preëminence, we
have but another proof of the imperishable
accuracy of wit. Only say a clever thing, and
mankind will go on forever furnishing living
illustrations of its truth. It was Thurlow who
originally remarked that " companies have neither bodies to kick nor souls to lose," and the
jest fits in so aptly with our every-day humors
and experiences that I have heard men attrib-
ute it casually to their friends, thinking, perhaps, that it must have been born in these
times of giant corporations, of city railroads,
and of trusts. What a gap between Queen
Victoria and Queen Bess, what a thorough and
far-reaching change in everything that goes to
make up the life and habits of men ; and yet
Shakespeare's fine strokes of humor have become so fitted to our common speech that the
very unconsciousness with which we apply
them proves how they tally with our modern
emotions and opportunities. Lesser lights
burn quite as steadily. Pope and Goldsmith
reappear on the lips of people whose knowledge of the " Essay on Man " is of the very
haziest character, and whose acquaintance with

"She Stoops to Conquer" is confined exclusively to Mr. Abbey's graceful illustrations.
Not very long ago I heard a bright school-girl,
when reproached for wet feet or some such
youthful indiscretion, excuse herself gayly
on the plea that she was "bullying Nature;"
and, knowing that the child was but modestly
addicted to her books, I wondered how many
of Dr. Holmes's trenchant sayings have become a heritage in our households, detached
often from their original kinship, and seeming like the rightful property of every one
who utters them.   It is an amusing, barefaced,
witless sort of robbery, yet surely not without
its compensations; for it must be a pleasant
thing to reflect in old age that the general
murkiness of life has been lit up here and
there by sparks struck from one's youthful
fire, and that these sparks, though they wan-
der occasionally masterless as will-o'-the-wisps,
are destined never to go out.

Are destined never to go out!   In its vitality lies the supreme excellence of humor.
Whatever has "wit enough to keep it sweet"
defies corruption and outlasts all time; but
the wit must be of that outward and visible

order which needs no introduction or demon-
stration at our hands.  It is an old trick with
dull novelists to describe their characters as
being exceptionally brilliant people, and to
trust that we will take their word for it, and
ask no further proof.  Every one remembers
how Lord Beaconsfield would tell us that a
cardinal could "sparkle with anecdote and
blaze with repartee;" and how utterly desti-
tute of sparkle or blaze were the specimens
of his eminence's conversation with which we
were subsequently favored.  Those "lively
dinners" in "Endymion" and "Lothair," at
which we were assured the brightest minds in
England loved to gather, became mere Barme-
cide feasts when reported to us without a single amusing remark; such waifs and strays of
conversation as reached our ears being of the
dreariest and most fatuous description.  It is
not so with the real masters of their craft.
Mr. Peacock does not stop to explain to us
that Dr. Folliott is witty.  The reverend gentleman opens his mouth and acquaints us with
the fact himself.  There is no need for George
Eliot to expatiate on Mrs. Poyser's humor.
Five minutes of that lady's society is amply

sufficient for the revelation. We do not even hear Mr. Poyser and the rest of the family enlarging delightedly on the subject, as do all of Lawyer Putney's friends, in Mr. Howells's story, " Annie Kilburn ; " and yet even the united testimony of Hatboro' fails to clear up our lingering doubts concerning Mr. Putney's wit. The dull people of that soporific town are really and truly and realistically dull. There is no mistaking them. The stamp of veracity is upon every brow. They pay morning calls, and we listen to their conversation with a dreamy impression that we have heard it all many times before, and that the ghosts of our own morning calls are revisiting us, not in the glimpses of the moon, but in Mr. Howells's decorous and quiet pages. That curious conviction that we have formerly passed through a precisely similar experience is strong upon us as we read, and it is the most emphatic testimony to the novelist's peculiar skill. But there is none of this instantaneous acquiescence in Mr. Putney's wit; for although he does make one very nice little joke, it is hardly enough to flavor all his conversation, which is for the most part rather unwholesome than humorous. The only way to elucidate him is to suppose that Mr. Howells, in sardonic mood, wishes to show us that if a man be discreet enough to take to hard drinking in his youth, before his general emptiness is ascertained, his friends invariably credit him with a host of shining qualities which, we are given to understand, lie balked and frustrated by his one unfortunate weakness. How many of us know these exceptionally brilliant lawyers, doctors, politicians, and journalists, who bear a charmed reputation, based exclusively upon their inebriety, and who take good care not to imperil it by too long a relapse into the mortifying self-revelations of soberness! And what wrong has been done to the honored name of humor by these pretentious rascals! We do not love Falstaff because he is drunk; we do not admire Becky Sharp because she is wicked. Drunkenness and wickedness are things easy of imitation; yet all the sack in Christendom could not beget us another Falstaff, — though Seithenyn ap Seithyn comes very near to the incomparable model, — and all the wickedness in the world could not fashion us a second Becky Sharp. There are too many dull topers and

stupid sinners among mankind to admit of
any uncertainty on those points.

Bishop Burnet, in describing Lord Halifax,
tells us, with thinly veiled disapprobation, that
he was " a man of fine and ready wit, full of
life, and very pleasant, but much turned to
satire. His imagination was too hard for his
judgment, and a severe jest took more with
him than all arguments whatever." Yet this
was the first statesman of his age, and one
whose clear and tranquil vision penetrated
so far beyond the turbulent, troubled times
he lived in, that men looked askance upon a
power they but dimly understood. The sturdy
" Trimmer," who would be bullied neither
by king nor commons, who would " speak his
mind and not be hanged as long as there was
law in England," must have turned with infinite relief from the horrible medley of plots
and counterplots, from the ugly images of
Oates and Dangerfield, from the scaffolds of
Stafford and Russell and Sidney, from the
Bloody Circuit and the massacre of Glencoe,
from the false smiles of princes and the howl-
ing arrogance of the mob, to any jest, however "severe," which would restore to him

his cold and fastidious serenity, and keep his judgment and his good temper unimpaired. " Ridicule is the test of truth," said Hazlitt, and it is a test which Halifax remorselessly applied, and which would not be without its uses to the Trimmer of to-day, in whom this adjusting sense is lamentably lacking. For humor distorts nothing, and only false gods are laughed off their earthly pedestals. What monstrous absurdities and paradoxes have resisted whole batteries of serious arguments, and then crumbled swiftly into dust before the ringing death-knell of a laugh! What healthy exultation, what genial warmth, what loyal brotherhood of mirth, attends the friendly sound! Yet in labeling our life and literature, as the Danes labeled their Royal Theatre in Copenhagen, " Not for amusement merely," we have pushed one step further, and the legend too often stands, " Not for amusement at all." Life is no laughing matter, we are told, which is true; and, what is still more dismal to contemplate, books are no laughing matters, either. Only now and then some gay, defiant rebel, like Mr. Saintsbury, flaunts the old flag, hums a bar of " Blue Bonnets over the Border," and ruffles the quiet waters of our souls by hinting that this age of Apollinaris and of lectures is at fault, and that it has produced nothing which can vie as literature with the products of the ages of wine and song.

In a fair and far-off country, hidden to none, though visited by few, dwell a little band of lovely ladies, to whose youth and radiance the poets have added the crowning gift of immortality. There they live, with faint alluring smiles that never fade ; and at their head is Helen of Troy, white-bosomed, azure-eyed, to whom men forgave all things for her beauty's sake. There, too, is Lesbia, fair and false, laughing at a broken heart, but holding close and tenderly the dead sparrow

"That, living, never strayed from her sweet breast."

She kisses its ruffled wings and weeps, she who had no tears to spare when Catullus sung and sued. And there is Myrto, beloved by Theocritus, her naked feet gleaming like pearls, a bunch of Coan rushes pressed in her rosy fingers ; and the nameless girl who held in check Anacreon's wandering heart with the magic of dimples, and parted lips,

and thin purple floating garments. With these
are later beauties: Fiammetta the ruddy-
haired, whom death snatched from Boccaccio's
arms, and the gentle Catarina, raising those
heavy-lidded eyes that Camoens loved and
lost; Petrarch's Laura, robed in pale green
spotted with violets, one golden curl escaping
wantonly beneath her veil; the fair blue-stock-
ing, Leonora d'Este, pale as a rain-washed
rose, her dress in sweet disorder; and Bea-
trice, with the stillness of eternity in her
brooding eyes. If we listen, we hear the shrill
laughter of Mignonne, a child of fifteen sum-
mers, mocking at Ronsard's wooing; or we
catch the gentler murmur of Highland Mary's
song. She blushes a little, the low-born
lass, and sinks her graceful head, as though
abashed by the fame her peasant lover brought
her. Barefooted, yellow-haired, she passes
swiftly by; and with her, hand in hand, walks
Scotland's queen, sad Jane Beaufort, "the
fairest younge floure" that ever won the heart
of royal captive and suffered the martyrdom
of love. England sends to that far land Stella,
with eyes like stars, and a veil of gossamer
hiding her delicate beauty, and Celia, and

false Lucasta, and Castara, tantalizingly discreet, in whose dimples Cupid is fain to linger
sighing, exiled, poor frozen god, from the

"Chaste nunnery of her breasts."

Sacharissa, too, stands near, with a shade of
listlessness in her sweet eyes, as though she
wearied a little of Master Waller's courtly
strains.  A withered rose droops from her
white fingers, preaching its mute sermon, and
preaching it all in vain; for rose and lady
live forever, linked to each other's fame.  And
by her side, casting her fragile loveliness in
the shade, is one of different mould, a sumptuous, smiling woman, on whom Sacharissa's
blue eyes fall with a soft disdain.  We know
this indolent beauty by the brave vibration
of her tempestuous silken robe, by the ruby
carcanet that clasps her throat, the rainbow
ribbon around her slender waist, the jewels
wedged knuckle-deep on every tapering finger,
and even — oh, vanity of vanities! — on one
small rosy thumb.  We know her by the
scented beads upon her arm, and by the sweet
and subtle odors of storax and spikenard and
galbanum that breathe softly forth from her

brocaded bodice, and from her hair's dark meshes caught in a golden net. It is she to whom the glow-worms lent their eyes, and the elves their wings, and the stars their shooting fires, as she wandered through the dewy woods to meet her lover's steps. It is Herrick's Julia whom we see so clearly through the mist of centuries, that cannot veil nor dim the brightness of her presence.

To ask how many of these fair dames have gone through the formality of living, and how many exist only by the might of a poet's breath, is but a thankless question. All share alike in that true being which may not be blown out like the flame of a taper; in that true entity which Cæsar and Hamlet hold in common, and which reveals them side by side. Mr. Gosse, for example, assures us that Julia really walked the earth, and even gives us some details of her mundane pilgrimage; other critics smile, and shake their heads, and doubt. It matters not; she lives, and she will continue to live when we who dispute the matter lie voiceless in our graves. The essence of her personality lingers on every page where Herrick sings of her. His verse is heavy with her spicy perfumes, glittering with her many-colored jewels, lustrous with the shimmer of her silken petticoats. Her very shadow, he sighs, distills sweet odors on the air, and draws him after her, faint with their amorous languor. How lavish she is with her charms, this woman who neither thinks nor suffers; who prays, indeed, sometimes, with great serenity, and dips her snowy finger in the font of blessed water, but whose spiritual humors pale before the calm vigor of her earthly nature! How kindly, how tranquil, how unmoved, she is; listening with the same slow smile to her lover's fantastic word-play, to the fervid conceits with which he beguiles the summer idleness, and to the frank and sudden passion with which he conjures her, " dearest of thousands," to close his eyes when death shall summon him, to shed some true tears above the sod, to clasp forever the book in which he writes her name! How gently she would have fulfilled these last sad duties had the discriminating fates called her to his bier; how fragrant the sighs she would have wafted in that darkened chamber; how sincere the temperate sorrow for a remediable

loss! And then, out into the glowing sunlight, where life is sweet, and the world exults, and the warm blood tingles in our veins,
and, underneath the scattered primrose blossoms, the frozen dead lie forgotten in their
graves.

What gives to the old love-songs their peculiar felicity, their undecaying brightness, is
this constant sounding of a personal note;
this artless candor with which we are taken
by the hand and led straight into the lady's
presence, are bidden to admire her beauty and
her wit, are freely reminded of her faults and
her caprices, and are taught, with many a
sigh and tear, and laughter bubbling throughout all, what a delicious and unprofitable pastime is the love-making of a poet.

"I lose but what was never mine,"

sings Carew with gay philosophy, contemplating the perfidious withdrawal of Celia's kind-
ness; and after worshiping hotly at her shrine,
and calling on all the winds of heaven to witness his desires, he accepts his defeat with
undimmed brow, and with melodious frankness
returns the false one her disdain : —

"No tears, Celia, now shall win
     My resolved heart to return;
I have searched thy soul within,
     And find naught but pride and scorn.
I have learned thy arts, and now
     Can disdain as much as thou."

From which heroic altitude we see him pres-
ently descending to protest with smiling lips
that love shall part with his arrows and the
doves of Venus with their pretty wings, that
the sun shall fade and the stars fall blinking
from the skies, that heaven shall lose its de-
lights and hell its torments, that the very fish
shall burn in the cool waters of the ocean, if
he forsakes or neglects his Celia's embraces.

It was Carew, indeed, who first sounded
these "courtly amorous strains" throughout
the English land; who first taught his fellow-
poets that to sing of love was not the occasional pastime, but the serious occupation of
their lives. Yet what an easy, indolent suitor
he is! What lazy raptures over Celia's eyes
and lips! What finely poised compliments,
delicate as rose leaves, and well fitted for the
inconstant beauty who listened, with faint
blushes and transient interest, to the song!
"He loved wine and roses," says Mr. Gosse,

"and fair florid women, to whom he could indite joyous or pensive poems about their comeliness, adoring it while it lasted, regretting it when it faded. He has not the same intimate love of detail as Herrick; we miss in his poetry those realistic touches that give such wonderful freshness to the verses of the younger poet; but the habit of the two men's minds was very similar. Both were pagans, and given up to an innocent hedonism; neither was concerned with much beyond the eternal commonplaces of bodily existence, the attraction of beauty, the mutability of life, the brevity and sweetness of enjoyment."

These things are quite enough, however, to make exceedingly good poets, Mrs. Browning to the contrary, notwithstanding. "I never mistook pleasure for the final cause of poetry, nor leisure for the hour of the poet," wrote the authoress of "Aurora Leigh," and we quail before the deadly earnestness of the avowal. But pleasure and leisure between them have begotten work far more complete and artistic than anything Mrs. Browning ever gave to an admiring world. Pleasure and leisure are responsible for "L'Allegro" and "Il Penseroso,"

for "Kubla Khan" and "The Eve of St. Agnes," for "Tam O'Shanter," and "A Dream
of Fair Women," and "The Bells." There is
so much talk about Herrick's paganism that it
has become one of the things we credit without
inquiry; shrugging our shoulders over Corinna
and her May blossoms, and passing by that
devout prayer of thanksgiving for the simple
blessings of life, for the loaf and the cup, the
winter hearthstone and the summer sun. There
is such a widely diffused belief in the necessity
for a serious and urgent motive in art that
we have grown to think less of the outward
construction of a poem than of the dominant
impulse which evoked it. Mrs. Browning,
with all her noble idealism and her profound
sense of responsibility, was most depressingly
indifferent about form, and was quite a law
to herself in the matter of rhymes. Carew,
whose avowed object was to flatter Celia and
Celia's fair rivals, proved himself "enamored
of perfection," and wrought with infinite care
and delicacy upon his fragile little verses. If
he only played at love-making, he was serious enough as a poet; and, amid the careless
exuberance of his time, he came to be re-

garded, like Flaubert some generations later, ·
as a veritable martyr to style. He brought
forth his lyrical children, complained Sir John
Suckling, with trouble and pain, instead of
with that light - hearted spontaneity which
distinguished his contemporaries, and which
made their poetry so deliciously easy to write,
and so generally unprofitable to read. Suckling himself, and Lovelace, and the host of
courtly writers who toyed so gracefully and so
joyously with their art, ignored for the most
part all severity of workmanship, and made it
their especial pride to compose with gentlemanly ease. The result may be seen in a
mass of half-forgotten rubbish, and in a few
incomparable songs, which are as fresh and
lovely to-day as when they first rang the
praises of Lucasta, or the fair Althea, or
Chloris,· the favorite daughter of wanton
Aphrodite. They are the models for all love-
songs and for all time, and, in their delicate
beauty, they endure like fragile pieces of por-
celain, to prove how light a thing can bear the
weight of immortality. We cannot surpass
them, we cannot steal their vivacious grace,
we cannot feel ourselves first in a field where

such delicious and unapproachable things have been already whispered.

> "Ah! frustrés par les anciens hommes,
> Nous sentons le regret jaloux,
> Qu'ils aient été ce que nous sommes,
> Qu'ils aient eu nos cœurs avant nous."

The best love-poems of the sixteenth and seventeenth centuries amply fulfill the requirements suggested by Southey : their sentiment is always "necessary, and voluptuous, and right." They are no "made-dishes at the Muses' banquet," but each one appears as the embodiment of a passing emotion. In those three faultless little verses "Going to the Wars," a single thought is presented us, — regretful love made heroic by the loyal farewell of the soldier suitor : —

> "Tell me not, sweet, I am unkind,
>   That from the nunnery
> Of thy chaste breast and quiet mind
>   To war and arms I flee.

> "True, a new mistress now I chase,
>   The first foe in the field,
> And, with a stronger faith, embrace
>   A sword, a horse, a shield.

> "Yet this inconstancy is such
>   As you too shall adore, —

I could not love thee, dear, so much,
Loved I not honour more."

In the still more beautiful lines, " To Althea
from Prison," passion, made dignified by suffering, rewards with lavish hand the captive,
happy with his chains : —

" If I have freedom in my love,
And in my soul am free,
Angels alone, that soar above,
Enjoy such liberty."

In both poems there is a tempered delicacy,
revealing the finer grain of that impetuous
soul which wrecked itself so harshly in the
stormy waters of life. Whether we think of
Lovelace as the spoiled darling of a voluptuous court, or as dying of want in a cellar;
whether we picture him as sighing at the feet
of beauty, or as fighting stoutly for his country
and his king; whether he is winning all hearts
by the resistless charms of voice and presence, or returning broken from battle to suffer
the bitterness of poverty and desertion, we
know that in his two famous lyrics we possess
the real and perfect fruit, the golden harvest,
of that troubled and many-sided existence.
A still smaller gleaning comes to us from Sir

Charles Sedley, who, for two hundred years, has been preserved from oblivion by a little wanton verse about Phillis, full of such good-natured contentment and disbelief that we grow young and cheerful again in contemplating it. Should any long-suffering reader desire to taste the sweets of sudden contrast and of sharp reaction, let him turn from the strenuous, analytic, half-caustic, and wholly discomforting love-poem of the nineteenth century — Mr. Browning's word-picture of " A Pretty Woman," for example — back to those swinging and jocund lines where Phillis,

" Faithless as the winds or seas,"

smiles furtively upon her suitor, whose clear-sightedness avails him nothing, and who plays the game merrily to the end : —

"She deceiving,
I believing,
What need lovers wish for more ? "

We who read are very far from wishing for anything more. With the Ettrick Shepherd, we are fain to remember that old tunes, and old songs, and well-worn fancies are best fitted for so simple and so ancient a theme : —

" A' the world has been in love at ae time
or ither o' its life, and kens best hoo to express its ain passion. What see you ever in
love-sangs that's at a' new ? Never ae single
word. It 's just the same thing over again,
like a vernal shower patterin' amang the bud-
din' words. But let the lines come sweetly,
and saftly, and a wee wildly too, frae the lips
of Genius, and they shall delight a' mankind,
and womankind too, without ever wearyin'
them, whether they be said or sung. But try
to be original, to keep aff a' that ever has been
said afore, for fear o' plagiarism, or in amb:.
tion o' originality, and your poem 'ill be like a
bit o' ice that you hae taken into your mouth
unawares for a lump o' white sugar."

Burns's unrivaled songs come the nearest,
perhaps, to realizing this charming bit of description ; and the Shepherd, anticipating
Schopenhauer's philosophy of love, is quite as
prompt as Burns to declare its promise sweeter
than its fulfillment : —

" Love is a soft, bright, balmy, tender, tri-
umphant, and glorious lie, in place of which
nature offers us in mockery, during a' the
rest o' our lives, the puir, paltry, pitiful,

fusionless, faded, cauldrified, and chittering substitute, Truth!"

This is not precisely the way in which we suffer ourselves nowadays to talk about truth, but a few generations back, people still cherished a healthy predilection for the comfortable delusions of life. Mingling with the music of the sweet old love-songs, lurking amid their passionate protestations, there is always a subtle sense of insecurity, a good-humored desire to enjoy the present, and not peer too closely into the perilous uncertainties of the future. Their very exaggerations, the quaint and extravagant conceits which offend our more exacting taste, are part of this general determination to be wisely blind to the ill-bred obtrusiveness of facts. Accordingly there is no staying the hand of an Elizabethan poet, or of his successor under the Restoration, when either undertakes to sing his lady's praises. Sun, moon, and skies bend down to do her homage, and to acknowledge their own comparative dimness.

"Stars, indeed, fair creatures be,"

admits Wither indulgently, and pearls and

rubies are not without their merits; but when
the beauty of Arete dawns upon him, all
things else seem dull and vapid by her side.
Nay, his poetry, even, is born of her complai-
sance, his talents are fostered by her smiles, he
gains distinction only as her favor may permit.

> " I no skill in numbers had,
> More than every shepherd's lad,
> Till she taught me strains that were
> Pleasing to her gentle ear.
> Her fair splendour and her worth
> From obscureness drew me forth.
> And, because I had no muse,
> She herself deigned to infuse
> All the skill by which I climb
> To these praises in my rhyme."

Donne, the most ardent of lovers and the
most crabbed of poets, who united a great devotion to his fond and faithful wife with a re-
markably poor opinion of her sex in general,
pushed his adulations to the extreme verge of
absurdity. We find him writing to a lady
sick of a fever that she cannot die because all
creation would perish with her, —

> " The whole world vapours in thy breath."

After which ebullition, it is hardly a matter

of surprise to know that he considered females in the light of creatures whom it had pleased Providence to make fools.

> "Hope not for mind in women!"

is his warning cry; at their best, a little sweetness and a little wit form all their earthly portion. Yet the note of true passion struck by Donne in those glowing addresses, those dejected farewells to his wife, echoes like a cry of rapture and of pain out of the stillness of the past. Her sorrow at the parting rends his heart; if she but sighs, she sighs his soul away.

> "When thou weep'st, unkindly kind,
>     My life's blood doth decay.
>         It cannot be
>     That thou lov'st me, as thou say'st,
>     If in thine my life thou waste;
>         Thou art the life of me."

Again, in that strange poem "A Valediction of Weeping," he finds her tears more than he can endure; and, with the fond exaggeration of a lover, he entreats forbearance in her grief : —

> "O more than moon,
> Draw not up seas to drown me in thy sphere;
> Weep me not dead in thine arms, but forbear

To teach the sea what it may do too soon.
Let not the wind example find
To do me more harm than it purposeth;
Since thou and I sigh one another's breath,
Whoe'er sighs most is cruellest, and hastes the other's
    death."

There is a lingering sweetness in these lines,
for all their manifest unwisdom, that is sur-
passed only by a pathetic sonnet of Drayton's,
where the pain of parting, bravely borne at
first, grows suddenly too sharp for sufferance,
and the lover's pride breaks and melts into
the passion of a last appeal : —

" Since there 's no helpe, — come, let us kisse and parte.
Nay, I have done, — you get no more of me ;
And I am glad, — yea, glad with all my hearte,
That thus so cleanly I myself can free.
Shake hands forever ! — cancel all our vows;
And when we meet at any time againe,
Be it not seene in either of our brows,
That we one jot of former love retaine.

" Now — at the last gaspe of Love's latest breath —
When, his pulse failing, passion speechless lies ;
When Faith is kneeling by his bed of death,
And Innocence is closing up his eyes,
Now ! if thou would'st — when all have given him
    over —
From death to life thou might'st him yet recover.''

Here, at least, we have grace of sentiment

and beauty of form combined to make a perfect whole. It seems strange indeed that Mr.
Saintsbury, who gives such generous praise to
Drayton's patriotic poems, his legends, his
epistles, even his prose prefaces, should have
no single word to spare for this most tender
and musical of leave-takings.

As for the capricious humors and over-
wrought imagery which disfigure so many of
the early love-songs, they have received their
full allotment of censure, and have provoked
the scornful mirth of critics too staid or too
sensitive to be tolerant. We hear more of
them, sometimes, than of the merits which
should win them forgiveness. Lodge, daz-
zled by Rosalynde's beauty, is ill disposed to
pass lightly over the catalogue of her charms.
Her lips are compared to budded roses, her
teeth to ranks of lilies ; her eyes are

" sapphires set in snow,
Refining heaven by every wink,"

her cheeks are blushing clouds, and her neck
is a stately tower where the god of love lies
captive. All things in nature contribute to
her excellence : —

" With Orient pearl, with ruby red,
   With marble white, with sapphire blue,
   Her body every way is fed,
   Yet soft to touch, and sweet in view."

But when this fair representative of all flowers and gems, "smiling to herself to think
of her new entertained passion," lifts up the
music of her voice in that enchanting madri-
gal,—

   " Love in my bosom, like a bee,
   Doth suck his sweet;
   Now with his wings he plays with me,
   Now with his feet," —

we know her at once for the kinswoman and
precursor of another and dearer Rosalind,
who, with boyish swagger and tell-tale grace,

   " like a ripe sister,"

gathers from the trees of Arden the first fruits
of Orlando's love. It was Lodge who pointed
the way to that enchanted forest, where exiles
and rustics waste the jocund hours, where toil
and care are alike forgotten, where amorous
verse-making represents the serious occupation of life, and where the thrice fortunate
Jaques can afford to dally with melancholy for
lack of any cankering sorrow at his heart.

William Habbington, who sings to us with
such monotonous sweetness of Castara's innocent joys, surpasses Lodge alike in the charm
of his descriptions and in the extravagance of
his follies. In reading him we are sharply
reminded of Klopstock's warning, that "a
man should speak of his wife as seldom and
with as much modesty as of himself;" for
Habbington, who glories in the fairness and
the chastity of his spouse, becomes unduly
boastful now and then in vaunting these perfections to the world. He, at least, being
safely married to Castara, feels none of that
haunting insecurity which disturbs his fellow-
poets.

> "All her vows religious be,
> And her love she vows to me,"

he says complacently, and then stops to assure
us in plain prose that she is "so unvitiated by
conversation with the world that the subtle-
minded of her sex would deem it ignorance."
Even to her husband-lover she is "thrifty of
a kiss," and in the marble coldness and purity
of her breast his glowing roses find a chilly
sepulchre. Cupid, perishing, it would seem,
from a mere description of her merits, or, as
Habbington singularly expresses it. —

"But if you, when this you hear,
Fall down murdered through your ear,"

is, by way of compensation, decently interred
in the dimpled cheek which has so often been
his lurking-place. Lilies and roses and violets exhale their odors around him, a beau-
teous sheet of lawn is drawn up over his cold
little body, and all who see the "perfumed
hearse " — presumably the dimple — envy the
dead god, blest in his repose. This is as bad
in its way as Lovelace's famous lines on " El-
linda's Glove," where that modest article of
dress is compelled to represent in turn a snow-
white farm with five tenements, whose fair
mistress has deserted them, an ermine cabinet
too small and delicate for any occupant but
its own, and a fiddle-case without its fine-
tuned instrument. Dr. Thomas Campion,
who, after rhyming delightfully all his life,
was pleased to write a treatise against that
" vulgar and artificial custom," compares his
lady's face, in one musical little song, to a fer-
tile garden, and her lips to ripe cherries,
which none may buy or steal because her eyes,
like twin angels, have them in keeping, and
her brows, like bended bows, defend such
treasures from the crowd.

" Those cherries fairly do enclose
　Of Orient pearl a double row,
Which, when her lovely laughter shows,
　They look like rose-buds filled with snow ;
Yet them nor peer nor prince can buy,
Till ' Cherry ripe ' themselves do cry."

This dazzling array of mixed metaphors
with which the early poets love to bewilder us,
and the whimsical conceits which must have
cost them many laborious hours, have at least
one redeeming merit: they are for the most
part illustrative of the lady's graces, and not
of the writer's lacerated heart.   They tell us,
seldom indeed with Herrick's intimate realism,
but with many quaint and suspicious exaggerations, whether the fair one was false or
fond, light or dark, serious or flippant, gentle
or high-spirited; what fashion of clothes she
wore, what jewels and flowers were her adornment: and these are the things we take pleasure in knowing.   It is Mr. Gosse's especial
grievance against Waller that he does not en-
lighten us on such points.   " We can form,"
he complains, " but a very vague idea of Lady
Dorothy Sidney from the Sacharissa poems ;
she is everywhere overshadowed by the poet
himself.   We are told that she can sleep

when she pleases, and this inspires a copy of
verses ; but later on we are told that she can
do anything but sleep when she pleases, and
this leads to another copy of verses, which
leave us exactly where we were when we
started." Indeed, those who express surprise
at Sacharissa's coldness have perhaps failed to
notice the graceful chill of her lover's poems.
"Cupid might have clapped him on the shoul-
der, but we could warrant him heart-whole."
For seven years he carried on his languid and
courtly suit without once warming to the passion point; and when Lady Dorothy at last
made up her mind to marry somebody else, he
expressed his cordial acquiescence in her views
in a most charming and playful letter to her
young sister, Lady Lucy Sidney, — a letter
containing just enough well-bred regret to
temper its wit and gayety. He had fulfilled
his part in singing the praises of his mistress,
in preaching to her sweetly through the soft
petals of a rose, and in sighing with gentle
complacency over the happy girdle which
bound her slender waist.

> " A narrow compass, and yet there
> Dwelt all that 's good, and all that 's fair ;

Give me but this ribbon bound
Take all the rest the sun goes round."

Here we have the prototype of that other
and more familiar cincture which clasped the
Miller's Daughter; and it must be admitted that Lord Tennyson's maiden, with her
curls, and her jeweled ear-rings, and the neck-
lace rising and falling all day long upon her
"balmy bosom," is more suggestive of a court
beauty, like the fair Sacharissa, than of a
buxom village girl.

The most impersonal, however, of all the
poet-lovers is Sir Philip Sidney, who, in the
hundred and eight sonnets dedicated to Stella,
has managed to tell us absolutely nothing
about her. The atmosphere of haunting indi-
viduality which gives these sonnets their half-
bitter flavor, and which made them a living
power in the stormy days of Elizabethan
poetry, reveals to us, not Stella, but Astrophel; not Penelope Devereux, but Sidney
himself, bruised by regrets and resentful of
his fate. They are not by any means passionate love-songs; they are not even sanguine
enough to be persuasive; they are steeped
throughout in a pungent melancholy, too rest-

less for resignation, too gentle for anger, too
manly for vain self-indulgence. In their delicacy and their languor we read the story of
that lingering suit which lacked the elation of
success and the heart-break of failure. Indeed, Sidney seems never to have been a very
ardent lover until the lady was taken away
from him and married to Lord Rich, when he
bewailed her musically for a couple of years,
and then consoled himself with Frances Wal-
singham, who must have found the sonnets to
her rival pleasant reading for her leisure
hours. This is the bald history of that poetic
passion which made the names of Stella and
Astrophel famous in English song, and which
stirred the disgust of Horace Walpole, whose
appreciation of such tender themes was of a
painfully restricted nature. In their thoughtful, introspective, and self-revealing character,
Sidney's love-poems bear a closer likeness to
the genius of the nineteenth than to that of
the sixteenth century. If we want to see the
same spirit at work, we have but to take up
the fifty sonnets by Dante Gabriel Rossetti,
called " The House of Life," wherein the
writer's soul is clearly reflected, but no glimpse

is vouchsafed us of the woman who has disturbed its depth.  Their vague, sweet pathos,
their brooding melancholy, their reluctant ac-
ceptance of a joyless mood, are all familiar
features in the earlier poet.  Such verses as
those beginning, —

> " Look in my face ; my name is Might-have-been ;
> I am also called No-more, Too-late, Farewell,"

are of the self-same mintage as Sidney's
golden coins, only more modern, and perhaps
more perfect in form, and a trifle more shadowy in substance.  If Sidney shows us but
little of Stella, and if that little is, judged by
the light of her subsequent career, not very
accurately represented, Rossetti far surpasses
him in unconscious reticence.  He is not un-
willing to analyze, — few recent poets are, —
but his analysis lays bare only the tumult of
his own heart, the lights and shades of his
own delicate and sensitive nature.

It was Sidney, however, who first pointed
out to women, with clear insistence, the advantage of having poets for lovers, and the
promise of immortality thus conferred on
them.  He entreats them to listen kindly to
those who can sing their praises to the world.

" For so doing you shall be most fair, most
wise, most rich, most everything ! You shall
feed upon superlatives." Carew, adopting the
same tone, and less gallant than Wither, who
refers even his own fame to Arete's kindling
glances, tells the flaunting Celia very plainly
that she owes her dazzling prominence to him
alone.

> " Know, Celia ! since thou art so proud,
> 'T was I that gave thee thy renown;
> Thou hadst in the forgotten crowd
> Of common beauties lived unknown,
> Had not my verse exhaled thy name,
> And with it impt the wings of fame."

What wonder that, under such conditions
and with such reminders, a passion for being be-rhymed seized upon all women, from
the highest to the lowest, from the marchion-
ess at court to the orange-girl smiling in the
theatre ! — a passion which ended its flutter-
ing existence in our great-grandmothers' al-
bums. Yet nothing is clearer, when we study
these poetic suits, than their very discouraging results. The pleasure that a woman takes
in being courted publicly in verse is a very
distinct sensation from the pleasure that she
expects to take when being courted privately

in prose. She is quick to revere genius, but
in her secret soul she seldom loves it. Genius, as Hazlitt scornfully remarks, "says such
things," and the average woman distrusts
"such things," and wonders why the poet will
not learn to talk and behave like ordinary people. It hardly needed the crusty shrewdness
of Christopher North to point out to us the
arrant ill-success with which the Muse has
always gone a-wooing. "Making love and
making love-verses," he explains, "are two of
the most different things in the world, and I
doubt if both accomplishments were ever found
highly united in the same gifted individual.
Inspiration is of little avail either to gods or
men in the most interesting affairs of life,
those of the earth. The pretty maid who
seems to listen kindly

'Kisses the cup, and passes it to the rest,'

and next morning, perhaps, is off before break-
fast in a chaise-and-four to Gretna Green,
with an aid-de-camp of Wellington, as desti-
tute of imagination as his master." It is the
cheerful equanimity with which the older poets
anticipated and endured some such finale as

this which gives them their precise advantage over their more exacting and self-centred successors.

For what is the distinctive characteristic of the early love-songs, and to what do they owe their profound and penetrating charm? It is that quality of youth which Heine so subtly recognized in Rossini's music, and which, to his world-worn ears, made it sweeter than more reflective and heavily burdened strains. Love was young when Herrick and Carew and Suckling went a-wooing; he has grown now to man's estate, and the burdens of manhood have kept pace with his growing powers. It is no longer, as at the feast of Apollo, a contest for the deftest kiss, but a life-and-death struggle in that grim arena where passion and pain and sorrow contend for mastery.

"Ah! how sweet it is to love!
Ah! how gay is young desire!"

sang Dryden, who, in truth, was neither sweet nor gay in his amorous outpourings, but who merely echoed the familiar sentiments of his youth. That sweetness and gayety of the past still linger, indeed, in some half-forgotten and wholly neglected verses which we have grown

too careless or too cultivated to recall. We
harden our hearts against such delicious trifling as

> " The young May moon is beaming, love,
> The glow-worm's lamp is gleaming, love."

We will have none of its pleasant moral, —

> " 'T is never too late for delight, my dear,"

and we will not even listen when Mr. Saintsbury tells us with sharp impatience that, in
turning our backs so coldly upon the poet who
enraptured our grandfathers, we are losing a
great deal that we can ill afford to spare.
The quality of youth is still more distinctly
discernible in some of Thomas Beddoes's dazzling little songs, stolen straight from the
heart of the sixteenth century, and lustrous
with that golden light which set so long ago.
It is not in spirit only, nor in sentiment, that
this resemblance exists; the words, the imagery, the swaying music, the teeming fancies
of the younger poet, mark him as one strayed
from another age, and wandering companion-
less under alien skies. Some two hundred
years before Beddoes's birth, Drummond of
Hawthornden, he who sang so tenderly the

praises of his sweet mistress, dead on her
wedding-day, wrote these quaint and pretty
lines entreating for her favor : —

> "I die, dear life, unless to me be given
> As many kisses as the Spring hath flowers,
> Or there be silver drops in Iris' showers,
> Or stars there be in all-embracing heaven.
> And if displeased, you of the match remain,
> You shall have leave to take them back again."

In Beddoes's unfinished drama of " Torres-
mond," we find Veronica's maidens singing her
to sleep with just such bright conceits and
soft caressing words, and their song rings
like an echo from some dim old room where
Lesbia, or Althea, or Celia lies a-dreaming: —

> " How many times do I love thee, dear ?
> Tell me how many thoughts there be
>         In the atmosphere
>         Of a new-fall'n year,
> Whose white and sable hours appear
> The latest flake of Eternity :
> So many times do I love thee, dear.

> " How many times do I love again ?
> Tell me how many beads there are
>         In a silver chain
>         Of evening rain,
> Unraveled from the tumbling main,
> And threading the eye of a yellow star:
> So many times do I love again."

It is not in this fairy fashion that the truly
modern poet declares his passion; it is not
thus that Wordsworth sings to us of Lucy,
the most alluring and shadowy figure in
English poetry, — Lucy, richly dowered with
a few short verses of unapproachable beauty.
To the lover of Wordsworth her death is a
lasting hurt.   We cannot endure to think of
her as he thinks of her, —

> " Rolled round in earth's diurnal course
> With rocks, and stones, and trees."

We cannot endure that anything so fine
and rare should slip forever from the sun-
shine, and that the secret stars should look
down upon her maidenhood no more.   Browning, too, who has been termed the poet of love,
who has revealed to us every changeful mood,
every stifled secret, every light and shade of
human emotion, — how has he dealt with his
engrossing theme?   Beneath his unsparing
touch, at once burning and subtle, the soul
lies bare, and its passions rend it like hounds.
All that is noble, generous, suffering, shameful, finds in him its ablest exponent.   Those
strange, fantastic sentences in which Mr. Pater has analyzed the inscrutable sorcery of

Mona Lisa, beneath whose weary eyelids "the thoughts and experiences of the world lie shadowed," might also fitly portray the image of Love, as Browning has unveiled him to our sight. He too is older than the rocks, and the secrets of the grave and of the deep seas are in his keeping. He too expresses all that man has come to desire in the ways of a thousand years, and his is the beauty " into which the soul with its maladies has passed." The slumbering centuries lie coiled beneath his feet, their hidden meaning is his to grasp, their huge and restless impulses have nourished him, their best results are his inheritance. But he is not glad, for the maladies of the soul have stilled his laughter, and the brightness of youth has fled.

# BOOKS THAT HAVE HINDERED ME.

So many grateful and impetuous spirits have recently come forward to tell to an approving world how they have been benefited by their early reading, and by their wisely chosen favorites in literature, that the trustful listener begins to think, against his own rueful experience, that all books must be pleasant and profitable companions. Those who have honored us with confidence in this matter seem to have found their letters, as Sir Thomas Browne found his religion, " all pure profit." Edward E. Hale, for instance, has been " helped " by every imaginable writer, from Marcus Aurelius to the amiable authoress of " The Wide, Wide World." Moncure D. Conway acknowledges his obligations to an infinite variety of sources. William T. Harris has been happy enough to seize instinctively upon those works which aroused his " latent energies to industry and self-activity ; " and Edward Eggleston has gathered

intellectual sustenance from the most unex-
pected quarters, — the Rollo Books, and Lind-
ley Murray's Reader. Only Andrew Lang
and Augustus Jessopp are disposed, with an
untimely levity, to confess that they have read
for amusement rather than for self-instruction,
and that they have not found it so easily at-
tainable.

Now when a man tells us that he has been
really " helped " by certain books, we naturally conclude that the condition reached by
their assistance is, in some measure, gratifying to himself; and, by the same token, I
am disposed to argue that my own unsatisfactory development may be the result of less
discreetly selected reading, — reading for
which, in many cases, I was wholly irrespon-
sible. I notice particularly that several persons who have been helped acknowledge a
very pleasing debt of gratitude to their early
spelling-books, to Webster's Elementary, and
to those modest volumes which first imparted
to them the mysteries of the alphabet. It was
not so with me. I learned my letters, at the
cost of infinite tribulation, out of a horrible
little book called " Reading Without Tears,"

which I trust has long since been banished
from all Christian nurseries. It was a brown
book, and had on its cover a deceptive picture
of two stout and unclothed Cupids holding
the volume open between them, and making
an ostentatious pretense of enjoyment. Young
as I was, I grew cynical over that title and
that picture, for the torrents of tears that I
shed blotted them both daily from my sight.
It might have been possible for Cupids, who
needed no wardrobes and sat comfortably on
clouds, to like such lessons, but for an ordinary little girl in frock and pinafore they
were simply heart-breaking. Had it only been
my good fortune to be born twenty years later,
spelling would have been left out of my early
discipline, and I should have found congenial
occupation in sticking pins or punching mysterious bits of clay at a kindergarten. But
when I was young, the world was still sadly
unenlightened in these matters; the plain
duty of every child was to learn how to read;
and the more hopelessly dull I showed myself to be, the more imperative became the
need of forcing some information into me, —
information which I received as responsively

as does a Strasbourg goose its daily share of provender. For two bitter years I had for my constant companion that hated reader, which began with such isolated statements as " Ann has a cat," and ended with a dismal story about a little African boy named Sam ; Mr. Rider Haggard not having then instructed us as to what truly remarkable titles little African boys enjoy. If, to this day, I am disposed to underrate the advantages of education, and to think but poorly of compulsory school-laws and the march of mind, it is because of the unhappy nature of my own early experiences.

Having at last struggled into some acquaintanceship with print, the next book to which I can trace a moral downfall is " Sandford and Merton," left on the nursery shelves by an elder brother, and read many times, not because I especially liked it, but because I had so little to choose from. Those were not days when a glut of juvenile literature had produced a corresponding indifference, and a spirit of languid hypercriticism. The few volumes we possessed, even those of a severely didactic order, were read and re-read, until we knew them well by heart. Now up

to a certain age I was, as all healthy children are, essentially democratic, with a de-
cided preference for low company, and a secret affinity for the least desirable little girls
in the neighborhood. But " Sandford and Merton " wrought a pitiable change. I do not
think I ever went so far as to dislike the Rev.
Mr. Barlow after the very cordial and hearty
fashion in which Dickens disliked him, and I
know I should have been scandalized by Mr.
Burnand's cheerful mockery ; but, pondering
over the matter with the stolid gravity of a
child, I reached some highly unsatisfactory
conclusions. It did not seem to me then, and
it does not seem to me now, exactly fair in the
estimable clergyman to have refused the board
which Mr. Merton was anxious to pay, and
then have reproached poor Tommy so coldly
with eating the bread of dependence ; neither
did it seem worth while for a wealthy little
boy to spend his time in doing — very ineffi-
ciently, I am sure — the work of an under-
gardener. Harry's contempt for riches, and
his supreme satisfaction with a piece of bread
for dinner, struck me as overdrawn ; Tommy's
mishaps were more numerous than need be,

even if he did have the misfortune to be a
gentleman's son ; and the complacency with
which Mr. Barlow permitted him to give away
a whole suit of clothes — clothes which, according to my childish system of ethics, be-
longed, not to him, but to his mother — con-
trasted but poorly with the anxiety manifested
by the reverend mentor over his own pitiful
loaf of bread. Altogether, " Sandford and
Merton " affected me the wrong way ; and for
the first time my soul revolted from the pretentious virtues of honest poverty. It is to
the malign influence of that tale that I owe
my sneaking preference for the drones and
butterflies of earth. I do not now believe that
men are born equal; I do not love universal
suffrage ; I mistrust all popular agitators, all
intrusive legislation, all philanthropic fads,
all friends of the people and benefactors of
their race. I cannot even sympathize with
the noble theory that every man and woman
should do their share of the world's work; I
would gladly shirk my own if I could. And
this lamentable, unworthy view of life and its
responsibilities is due to the subtle poison
instilled into my youthful mind by the too

streuuous counter-teaching of "Sandford and Merton."

A third pitfall was dug for my unwary feet when, as a school-girl of fifteen, I read, sorely against my will, Milton's "Areopagit-ica." I believe this is a work highly esteemed by critics, and I have even heard people in private life, who might say what they pleased without scandal, speak quite enthusiastically of its manly spirit and sonorous rhetoric. Perhaps they had the privilege of reading it skippingly to themselves, and not as I did, aloud, paragraph after paragraph, each weighted with mighty sentences, cumbrous, involved, majestic, and, so far as my narrow comprehension went, almost unintelligible. Never can I forget the aspect of those pages, bristling all over with mysterious allusions to unknown people and places, and with an armed phalanx of Greek and Roman names which were presumably familiar to my in-structed mind, but which were really dug out bodily from my Classical Dictionary, at the cost of much time and temper. I have counted in one paragraph, and that a moder-ately short one, forty-five of these stumbling-

blocks, ranging all the way from the "libertine school of Cyrene," about which I knew
nothing, to the no less libertine songs of Naso,
about which I know nothing now. Neither
was it easy to trace the exact connection between the question at issue, "the freedom of
unlicenc'd printing," and such far-off matters
as the gods of Egypt and the comedies of Plautus, Isaiah's prophecies and the Carthaginian
councils. Erudition, like a bloodhound, is a
charming thing when held firmly in leash,
but it is not so attractive when turned loose
upon a defenseless and unerudite public.
Lady Harriet Ashburton used to say that,
when Macaulay talked, she was not only inun-
dated with learning, but she positively stood
in the slops. In reading Milton, I waded
knee-deep, utterly out of my element, and
deeply resentful of the experience. The liberty of the press was, to my American notions,
so much a matter of course, that the only way
I could account for the continued withholding
of so commonplace a privilege was by suppos-
ing that some unwary members of Parliament
read the "Areopagitica," and were forthwith
hardened into tyranny forever. I own I felt

a savage glee in reflecting that Lords and Commons had received this oppressive bit of literature in the same aggrieved spirit that I had myself, and that its immediate result was to put incautious patriots in a more ticklish position than before.   If truth now seems to me a sadly overrated virtue ; if plain-speaking is sure to affront me ; if the vigorous personalities of the journalist and the amiable indecencies of the novel-writer vex my illiberal soul, and if the superficial precautions of a paternal government appear estimable in my eyes, to what can I trace this alien and unprogressive attitude, if not to the " Areopagitica," and its adverse influence over my rebellious and suffering girlhood ?

As these youthful reminiscences are of too mournful a nature to be profitably prolonged, I will add only two more to the list of books which have hindered my moral and intellectual development.   When I was seventeen, I read, at the earnest solicitation of some well-meaning friends, " The Heir of Redclyffe," and my carefully guarded theories of life shivered and broke before the baneful lesson it conveyed.   Brought up on a comfortable and

wholesome diet of Miss Edgeworth's pleasant
stories, I had unconsciously absorbed the genial doctrine that virtue is its own reward,
and that additional rewards are sure to be
forthcoming; that happiness awaits the good
and affable little girl, and that well-merited
misfortunes dog the footsteps of her who in-
clines to evil ways. I trusted implicitly to
those shadowy mills where the impartial gods
grind out our just deserts; and the admirable
songs in "Patience" about Gentle Jane and
Teasing Tom inadequately express the rigidity of my views and the boundless nature of
my confidence. "The Heir of Redclyffe" destroyed, at once and forever, this cheerful
delusion, and with it a powerful stimulus to
rectitude. Here are Sir Guy Morville and
poor little Amy, both of them virtuous to a
degree which would have put Miss Edgeworth's most exemplary characters to the
blush; yet Guy, after being bullied and
badgered through the greater part of his short
life, dies of the very fever which should properly have carried off Philip; and Amy, besides being left widowed and heart-broken,
gives birth to a daughter instead of a son,

and so forfeits the inheritance of Redclyffe.
On the other hand, Philip, the most intoler-
able of prigs and mischief-makers, whose cruel
suspicions play havoc with the happiness of
everybody in the story, and whose obstinate
folly brings about the final disaster, — Philip,
who is little better than his cousin's murderer,
succeeds to the estate, marries that very stilted
and unpleasant young person, Laura (who is
after all a world too good for him), and is
left in a blaze of glory, a wealthy, honored,
and distinguished man.   It is true that Miss
Yonge, whose conscience must have pricked
her a little at bringing about this unwarranted
and unjustifiable conclusion, would have us
believe that he was sorry for his misbehavior,
and that his regret was sufficient to equalize
the perfidious scales of justice; but even at
seventeen I was not guileless enough to credit
the lasting quality of Philip's contrition.   A
very few years would suffice to reconcile him to
Guy's death, and to convince him that his own
succession was a mere survival of the fittest, an
admirable intervention on the part of Destiny
to remedy her former blunders, and exalt him
to his proper station in the world.   But to

me this triumph of guilt meant the downfall of my early creed, the destruction of my most cherished convictions. Never again might I look forward with hopeful heart to the inevitable righting of all wrong things ; never again might I trust with old-time confidence to the final readjustment of a closing chapter. Even Emerson's essay on "Compensation" has failed to restore to me the full measure of all that I lost through the "The Heir of Redclyffe."

The last work to injure me seriously as a girl, and to root up the good seed sown in long years of righteous education, was "Uncle Tom's Cabin," which I read from cover to cover with the innocent credulity of youth ; and, when I had finished, the awful conviction forced itself upon me that the thirteenth amendment was a ghastly error, and that the war had been fought in vain. Slavery, which had seemed to me before undeviatingly wicked, now shone in a new and alluring light. All things must be judged by their results, and if the result of slavery was to produce a race so infinitely superior to common humanity ; if it bred strong, capable, self-

restrained men like George, beautiful, coura-
geous, tender-hearted women like Eliza, vi-
sions of innocent loveliness like Emmeline;
marvels of acute intelligence like Cassy, children of surpassing precocity and charm like
little Harry, mothers and wives of patient,
simple goodness like Aunt Chloe, and, finally,
models of all known chivalry and virtue like
Uncle Tom himself, — then slavery was the
most ennobling institution in the world, and
we had committed a grievous crime in de-
grading a whole heroic race to our narrower,
viler level. It was but too apparent, even to
my immature mind, that the negroes whom I
knew, or knew about, were very little better
than white people; that they shared in all the
manifold failings of humanity, and were not
marked by any higher intelligence than their
Caucasian neighbors. Even in the matters
of physical beauty and mechanical ingenuity
there had plainly been some degeneracy, some
falling off from the high standard of old slavery days. Reluctantly I concluded that what
had seemed so right had all been wrong indeed, and that the only people who stood pre-
eminent for virtue, intellect, and nobility had

been destroyed by our rash act, had sunk under the enervating influence of freedom to a range of lower feeling, to baser aspirations and content. It was the greatest shock of all, and the last.

I will pursue the subject no further. Those who read these simple statements may not, I fear, find them as edifying or as stimulating as the happier recollections of more favored souls; but it is barely possible that they may see in them the unvarnished reflection of some of their own youthful experiences.

THERE is a delightful little story, very well told by Mr. James Payn, the novelist, about an unfortunate young woman who for years concealed in her bosom the terrible fact that she did not think " John Gilpin " funny ; and who at last, in an unguarded moment, confessed to him her guilty secret, and was promptly comforted by the assurance that, for his part, he had always found it dull. The weight that was lifted from that girl's mind made her feel for the first time that she was living in an age which tolerates freedom of conscience, and in a land where the Holy Office is unknown. It is only to be feared that her newly acquired liberty inclined her to be as much of a Philistine as Mr. Payn himself, and to believe, with him, that all orthodoxy is of necessity hypocritical, and that when a man says he admires the " Faerie Queene," or " Paradise Lost," or Rabelais, the chances are that he knows little or nothing

about them. Now, as a matter of fact, it is seldom safe to judge others too rigidly by our own
inadequate standards, or to assume that because we prefer " In Memoriam " to " Lycidas,"
our friend is merely adopting a tone of grievous superiority when he modestly but firmly
asserts his preference for the earlier dirge. It
is even possible that although we may find
" Don Quixote " dull, and " The Excursion "
vapid, another reader, no whit cleverer, we are
sure, than ourselves, may enjoy them both, with
honest laughter and with keen delight. There
is doubtless as much affectation in the world
of books as in the worlds of art and fashion ;
but there must always be a certain proportion
of men and women who, whether by natural
instinct or acquired grace, derive pleasure
from the highest ranks of literature, and who
should in common justice be permitted to say
so, and to return thanks for the blessings ac-
corded them. " It is in our power to think
as we will," says Marcus Aurelius, and it
should be our further privilege to give unfet-
tered expression to our thoughts.

Nevertheless, human nature is weak and
erring, and the pitfalls dug for us by wily

critics are baited with the most ensnaring devices.  It is not the great writers of the world
who have the largest following of sham admirers, but rather that handful of choice
spirits who, we are given to understand, appeal only to a small and chosen band.  Few
of us find it worth our while to pretend a passionate devotion for Shakespeare, or Milton,
or Dante.  On the contrary, nothing is more
common than to hear people complain that the
"Inferno " is unpleasant, and "Paradise Lost "
dreadfully long, neither of which charges is
easily refutable in terms.  But when we read
in a high-class review that " just as Spenser is
the poet's poet, so Peacock is the delight of
critics and of wits ; " or that " George Meredith, writing as he does for an essentially cultivated and esoteric audience, has won but a
limited recognition for his brilliant group of
novels ; " or that " the subtle and far-reaching
excellence of Ibsen's dramatic work is a quality
absolutely undecipherable to the groundlings,"
who can resist tendering his allegiance on the
spot ?  It is not in the heart of man to harden
itself against the allurements of that magic
word " esoteric," nor to be indifferent to the

distinction it conveys. Mr. Payn, indeed, in a robust spirit of contradiction, has left it on record that he found "Headlong Hall" and "Crotchet Castle" intolerably dull; but this I believe to have been an unblushing falsehood, in the case of the latter story, at least. It is hardly within the bounds of possibility that a man blessed with so keen a sense of humor could have found the Rev. Dr. Folliott dull; but it is quite possible that the average reader, whose humorous perceptions are of a somewhat restricted nature, should find Mr. Peacock enigmatic, and the oppressive brilliancy of Mr. Meredith's novels a heavy load to bear. There is such a thing as being intolerably clever, and "Evan Harrington" and "The Egoist" are fruitful examples of the fact. The mind is kept on a perpetual strain, lest some fine play of words, some elusive witticism, should be disregarded; the sense of continued effort paralyzes enjoyment; fatigue provokes in us an ignoble spirit of contrariety, and we sigh perversely for that serene atmosphere of dullness which in happier moments we affected to despise.

"A man," says Dr. Johnson bluntly, " ought

to read just as inclination leads him, for what he reads as a task will do him little good." In other words, if his taste is for Mr. Rider Haggard's ingenious tales, it is hardly worth his while to pretend that he prefers Tolstoï. His more enlightened brother will indeed pass him by with a shiver of pained surprise, but he has the solid evidence of the booksellers to prove that he is not sitting alone in his darkness. Yet nowadays the critic diverts his heaviest scorn from the guilty author, who does not mind it at all, to the sensitive reader, who minds it a great deal too much; and the result is that cowardice prompts a not unnatural deception. Few of us remember what Dr. Johnson chanced to say on the subject, and fewer still are prepared to solace ourselves with his advice; but when an unsparing disciplinarian like Mr. Frederic Harrison lays down the law with a chastening hand, we are all of us aroused to a speedy and bitter consciousness of our deficiencies. "The incorrigible habit of reading little books" — a habit, one might say, analogous to that of eating common food — meets with scant tolerance at the hands of this inexorable reformer. Bet-

ter, far better, never to read at all, and so
keep the mind "open and healthy," than be
betrayed into seeking "desultory information"
from the rank and file of literature. To
be simply entertained by a book is an unpar-
donable sin ; to be gently instructed is very
little better. In fact, Mr. Harrison carries
his severity to such a pitch that, on reach-
ing this humiliating but comforting sentence,
" Systematic reading, in its true sense, is
hardly possible for women," it was with a
feeble gasp of relief that I realized our igno-
minious exclusion from the race. I do not
see *why* systematic reading should be hardly
possible for women, any more than I see what
is to become of Mr. Harrison if we are to give
up little books, but never before did the limitations of sex appear in so friendly a light.
There is something frightful in being required
to enjoy and appreciate all masterpieces; to
read with equal relish Milton, and Dante, and
Calderon, and Goethe, and Homer, and Scott,
and Voltaire, and Wordsworth, and Cervantes, and Molière, and Swift. One is irresistibly reminded of Mrs. Blimber surveying
the infant Paul Dombey. " Like a bee," she

murmured, "about to plunge into a garden of
the choicest flowers, and sip the sweets for the
first time. Virgil, Horace, Ovid, Terence,
Plautus, Cicero. What a world of honey have
we here ! " And what a limited appetite and
digestion awaited them! After all, these great
men did not invariably love one another, even
when they had the chance. Goethe, for instance, hated Dante, and Scott very cordially
disliked him ; Voltaire had scant sympathy
with "Paradise Lost," and Wordsworth fo-
cused his true affection upon the children of
his own pen.

It is very amusing to see the position now
assigned by critics to that arch - offender,
Charles Lamb, who, himself the idlest of
readers, had no hesitation in commending the
same unscrupulous methods to his friends.
We are told in one breath of his unerring literary judgment, and, in the next, are solemnly
warned against accepting that judgment as
our own. He is the most quoted, because the
most quotable of writers, yet every one who
uses his name seems faintly displeased at hearing it upon another's lips. I have myself
been reminded with some sharpness, by a re-

viewer, that illustrations drawn from Lamb counted for nothing in my argument, because his was " a unique personality," a " pure imagination, which even the drama of the Restoration could not pollute." But this seems to be assuming more than we have any right to assume. I cannot take it upon myself to say, for example, that Mr. Bagehot's mind was more susceptible to pollution than Charles Lamb's. I am not sufficiently in the secrets of Providence to decide upon so intimate and delicate a question. But granted that others have a clearer light on these matters than I have, it would still appear as though the unpolluted source were the best from which to draw one's help and inspiration. What really makes Lamb a doubtful guide through the mazes of literature is the fact that there is not a single rule given us in these sober days for the proper administration of our faculties which he did not take a positive pleasure in transgressing. His often-quoted heresy in regard to those volumes which " no gentleman's library should be without " might perhaps be spared the serious handling it receives ; but his letters abound in passages equally shame-

less and perverting. "I feel as if I had read
all the books I want to read," he writes un-
concernedly; and again, "I take less pleasure
in reading than heretofore, but I like books
about books." And so, alas! do we; though
this is the most serious charge laid at our
doors, and one which has subjected us to the
most humiliating reproofs. It is very pleasant
to have Mr. Ainger tell us what an admirable
critic Lamb was, and with what unerring cer-
tainty he pointed out the best lines of Wordsworth and Southey and Coleridge. The fact
remains — though to this Mr. Ainger does
not draw our attention — that he found nothing to praise in Byron, heartily disliked
Shelley, never, so far as we can see, read
Keats, condemned Faust unhesitatingly as "a
disagreeable, canting tale of seduction," and
discovered strong points of resemblance between Southey and Milton. Under these circumstances, it is hardly safe to elect him as a
critical fetich, if we feel the need of such an article, merely because he admired the "Ancient
Mariner" and Blake's "Chimney Sweeper,"
and did not particularly admire "We are
Seven." Even his fine and subtle sympathy

with Shakespeare is a thing to be revered and
envied, rather than analyzed and drawn into
service, where it will answer little purpose. But
what is none the less sure is that Lamb recognized by a swift and delicate intuition the literary food that was best fitted to nourish his
own intellectual growth. This was Sir Walter Scott's secret, and this was Lamb's. Both
knew instinctively what was good for them,
and a clear perception of our individual needs
is something vastly different from idle preference based on an ignorant conceit. It is
what we have each of us to learn, if we would
hope to thrive ; and while we may be aided in
the effort, yet a general command to read and
enjoy all great authors seldom affords us the
precise assistance we require.

Still less do we derive any real help from
those more contentious critics who, being
wedded hard and fast to one particular author
or to one particular school of thought, refuse,
with ostentatious continency, to cast lingering
looks upon any other type of loveliness. Literary monogamy, as practiced by some of our
contemporaries, makes us sigh for the old genial days of Priest Martin, when the tyranny

of opinions had not yet grown into a binding
yoke, and when it was still possible to follow
the example of Montaigne's old woman, and
light one candle to Saint Michael and another
to the Dragon. At present, the saint — or
perhaps the dragon — stands in a blaze of
glory, all the more lustrous for the dark
shadow thrown on his antagonist. "Praise
handed in by disparagement," the Greek drama
whipped upon the back of Genesis, — if I
may venture to quote Charles Lamb again —
this is the modern method of procedure, a
method successfully inaugurated by Macaulay,
who could find no better way of eulogizing
Addison than by heaping antithetical reproaches upon Steele. In a little volume of
lectures upon Russian literature, lectures
which were sufficiently popular to bear both
printing and delivery, I find the art of per-
suasiveness illustrated by this firebrand of a
sentence, hurled like an anathema at the heads
of a peaceful and unoffending community :
"Read Tolstoï! Read humbly, read admir-
ingly! Reading him in this spirit shall in
itself be unto you an education of your highest
artistic nature. And when your souls have

become able to be thrilled to their very depths
by the unspeakable beauty of Tolstoï's art,
you will then learn to be ashamed of the
thought that for years you sensible folks of
Boston have been capable of allowing the Ste-
vensons with their Hydes, and the Haggards
with their Shes, and even the clumsy Wards
with their ponderous Elsmeres, to steal away,
under the flag of literature, your thoughtful
moments."

Now, apart from the delightful vagueness of
perspective, — for "Robert Elsmere" and
"She" grouping themselves amicably together
is a spectacle too pleasant to be lost, — I cannot but think that there is something oppressive about the form in which these comments
are offered to the world. It reminds one of
that highly dramatic scene in Bulwer's "Riche-
lieu," where the aged cardinal hurls "the curse
of Rome" at a whole stageful of people, who
shrink and cower without knowing very distinctly at what. Why should critics, I wonder, always adopt this stringent and defiant
tone when they would beguile us to the enjoyment of Russian fiction? Why should the
reading of Tolstoï necessarily imply a con-

tempt for Robert Louis Stevenson? Why,
when we have been "thrilled to our very
depths" by "Peace and War" or "Anna
Karenina," should we not devote a few spare
moments to the consideration of "Markheim,"
a story whose solemn intensity of purpose in
no way mars its absolute and artistic beauty?
And why, above all, should we be petulantly
reprimanded, like so many stupid and obstinate children? I cannot even think that Mr.
Howells is justified in calling the English
nation "those poor islanders," as if they
were dancing naked somewhere in the South
Seas, merely because they love George Eliot
and Thackeray as well as Jane Austen.
They love Jane Austen too. We all love
her right heartily, but we have no need to emulate good Queen Anne, who, as Swift ob-
served, had not a sufficient stock of amity for
more than one person at a time. We may
not, indeed, be prepared to say with Mr.
Howells that Miss Austen is "the first and
the last of the English novelists to treat mate-
rial with entire truthfulness," having some
reasonable doubts as to the precise definition
of truth. We may not care to emphasize our

affection for her by repudiating with one
breath all her great successors. We may not
even consider " The Newcomes " and "Henry
Esmond" as illustrating the degeneracy of
modern fiction ; yet nevertheless we may enjoy some fair half-hours in the company of
Emma Woodhouse and Mr. Elton, of Catherine Morland and Elizabeth Bennet. Only,
when we are searching for a shibboleth by
which to test our neighbor's intellectual worth,
let not Jane Austen's be the name, lest we be
rewarded for our trouble by hearing the faint,
clear ripple of her amused laughter — that
gentle, feminine, merciless laughter — echoing
softly from the dwelling-place of the immortals.

It is inevitable, moreover, that too much
rigidity on the part of teachers should be followed by a brisk spirit of insubordination
on the part of the taught. Accordingly, now
and then, some belligerent freeman rushes
into print, and shakes our souls by declaring
breathlessly that he hates " Wagner, and Mr.
Irving, and the Elgin Marbles, and Goethe,
and Leonardo da Vinci ; " and this rank
socialism in literature and art receives a very
solid and shameless support from the more

light-minded writers of the day. Mr. Birrell, for instance, fails to see why the man who liked Montgomery's poetry should have been driven away from it by Macaulay's stormy rhetoric, nor why Macaulay himself could not have let poor Montgomery alone, nor why " some cowardly fellow" should join in the common laugh at Tupper, when he knows very well that in his secret soul he much prefers the " Proverbial Philosophy " to " Atalanta in Calydon " or " Empedocles on Etna." A recent contributor to Macmillan assures us, with discouraging candor, that it is all vanity to educate ourselves into admiring Turner, and that it is not worth while to try and like the " Mahabharata " or the " Origin of Species," if we really enjoy " King Solomon's Mines " or the " Licensed Victualler's Gazette." On the other hand, we have Ruskin's word for it that unless we love Turner with our whole hearts we shall not be — artistically speaking — saved ; and hosts of strenuous critics in the field of letters are each and every one assuring us that there is no intellectual future for the world unless we speedily tender our allegiance wherever he says it is due.

Poet-censors, like Mr. Swinburne, whose words are bitterness and whose charity is small, lay crooked yokes upon our galled necks. Even the story-tellers have now turned reviewers on their own account, and gravely tell us how many novels, besides their own, we should feel ourselves at liberty to read.

Under these circumstances, it is hardly a matter of surprise that people whose minds are, as Mr. Bagehot termed it, "to let" stand hesitating between license and servitude. On the one side, we hear men — intelligent men, too — boasting that they never read anything but the newspapers, and seeming to take a perverted pride in their own melancholy deprivation. On the other, we see both men and women, and sometimes even children, practicing a curious sort of literary asceticism, and devoting themselves conscientiously and very conspicuously to the authors they least enjoy. These martyrs to an advanced culti- vation find their self-imposed tasks, I am happy to think, grow harder year by year. Helen Pendennis, occasionally reading Shake- speare, "whom she pretended to like, but did n't," had comparatively an easy time of

it; but her successor to-day who goes to a
lecture on Hegel or Euripides when she would
prefer cards and conversation; who sits, per-
plexed and doubtful, through a performance
of "A Doll's House" when "Little Lord
Fauntleroy" represents her dramatic preference; who tries to read Matthew Arnold and
Tourguéneff, and now and then Mr. Pater,
when she really enjoys Owen Meredith,
and "Bootles' Baby," and the Duchess,
pays a heavy price for her enviable reputation
"The true value of souls is in proportion to
what they can admire," says Marius the
Epicurean; but the true value of our friends'
distinction is in proportion to the books we
behold in their hands. We have hardly yet
outgrown the critical methods of the little
heroine of "Mademoiselle Panache," who
knows that Lady Augusta is accomplished
because she has seen her music and heard of
her drawings; and, as few of us resemble
the late Mr. Mark Pattison in his unwilling-
ness to create a good impression, we naturally
make an effort to be taken at our best. Mr.
Payn once said that Macaulay had frightened
thousands into pretending they knew authors

with whom they had not even a bowing acquaintance; and though the days of his au-
tocracy are over, it has been succeeded by
a more fastidious and stringent legislation.
We no longer feel it incumbent upon us to
profess an intimacy with Thucydides, nor to
revere the " Pilgrim's Progress." Indeed, a
recent critic has been found brave enough to
speak harsh words concerning the Delectable
Mountains and the Valley of Humiliation, —
words that would have frozen the current of
Macaulay's blood, and startled even the tolerant Sainte-Beuve, weary as he confessed
himself of the Pilgrim's vaunted perfections.
But there is always a little assortment of
literary shibboleths, whose names we con over
with careful glibness, that we may assert our
intimacy in hours of peril; nor should we,
in justice, be censured very severely for doing
what is too often with us, as with the Ephra-
imites, a deed of simple self-defense.

These passwords of culture, although their
functions remain always the same, vary
greatly with each succeeding generation;
and, as they make room in turn for one another, they give to the true and modest lovers

of an author a chance to enjoy him in peace.
Wordsworth is now, for example, the cherished friend of a tranquil and happy band,
who read him placidly in green meadows or
by their own firesides, and forbear to trouble
themselves about the obstinate blindness of
the disaffected. But there was a time when
battles royal were fought over his fame, owing
principally, if not altogether, to the insulting
pretensions of his followers. It was then considered a correct and seemly thing to vaunt
his peculiar merits, as if they reflected a shadowy grandeur upon all who praised them,
very much in the spirit of the little Austra-
lian boy who said to Mr. Froude, "Don't
you think the harbor of Sydney does us great
credit?" To which the historian's characteristic reply was, "It does, my dear, if you made
it." Apart from the prolonged and point-
less discussion of Wordsworth's admirable
moral qualities, "as though he had been the
candidate for a bishopric," there was always
a delicately implied claim on the part of his
worshipers that they possessed finer perceptions than their neighbors, that they were in
some incomprehensible way open to influences

which revealed nothing to less subtle and discriminating souls. The same tone of heart-
felt superiority is noticeable among the very
ardent admirers of Robert Browning, who
seem to be perpetually offering thanks to
Heaven that they are not as other men, and
who evince a gentle but humiliating contempt
for their uninitiated fellow-creatures ; while
Ibsen's fervent devotees dwell on the mountain tops apart. How many people, I wonder,
who believe that they have loved Shelley all
their lives, find themselves exceedingly dazed
and harassed by what Mr. Freeman calls " the
snares of Shelleyana," a mist of confusing
chatter and distorted praise! How many un-
ambitious readers, who would fain enjoy their
Shakespeare quietly, are pursued even to their
peaceful chimney-corners by the perfidious
devices of commentators and of cranks! In
the mean while, an experienced few ally themselves, with supreme but transient enthusiasm,
to Frédéric Mistral or to Pushkin, to Omar
Khayyám or to Amiel ; and an inexperienced
many strive falteringly to believe that they
were acquainted with the Rubáiyát before the
date of Mr. Vedder's illustrations, and that

the diary of a half-Germanized Frenchman,
submerged in a speculative and singularly
cheerless philosophy, represents the intellectual food for which their souls are craving.

The object of criticism, it has been said, is
to supply the world with a basis, a definition
which cannot be accused of lacking sufficient
liberality and breadth. Yet, after applying
the principle for a good many years, it is discouraging to note that what has really been
afforded us is less a basis than a battlefield,
the din and tumult from which strike a dis-
cordant note in our lives. That somewhat
contemptuous severity with which critics ad-
dress the general public, and which the general public very stoutly resents, is urbanity
itself when compared with the language which
they feel themselves privileged to use to one
another. Señor Armando Palacio Valdés, for
example, who has been recently presented to
us as a clear beacon-light to guide our wandering steps, has no hesitation in saying that
" among the vulgar, *of course*," he includes
"the greater part of those who write literary
criticism, and who constitute the worst vulgar,
since they teach what they do not know."

But this is the kind of thing that is very easy
to say, and carries no especial weight when
said. The "of course" adds, indeed, a faint
flavor of unconscious humor to the enviable
complacency of the whole, and there is always
a certain satisfaction to a generous soul in the
sight of a fellow-mortal so thoroughly enjoying the altitude to which he believes he has
risen.

> "Let us sit on the thrones
> In a purple sublimity,
> And grind down men's bones
> To a pale unanimity,"

sings Mrs. Browning in one of her less luminous moments; and Señor Valdés and his
friends respond with alacrity, "We will!"
Unhappily, however, "the greater part of
those who write literary criticism," while perhaps no more vulgar than their neighbors, are
not generous enough nor humorous enough to
appreciate the delicate irony of the situation.
They rush forward to protest with energetic
ill temper, and the air is dark with warfare.
Alas for those who succeed, as Montaigne ob-
served, in giving to their harmless opinions a
fatal air of importance! Alas for those who

tilt with irrational chivalry at all that man
holds dear! How many years have passed
since Saint-Evremond uttered his cynical protest against the unprofitable wisdom of reformers; and to-day, when one half the world
devotes itself strenuously to the correction and
improvement of the other half, what is the
result, save pretense, and contention, and a
dismal consciousness of insecurity! More
and more do we sigh for greater harmony and
repose in the intellectual life ; more and more
do we respect the tranquil sobriety of that
wise old worldling, Lord Chesterfield, who
counsels every man to think as he pleases, or
rather as he can, but to forbear to disclose his
valuable ideas when they are of a kind to dis-
turb the peace of society.

In reading the recently published letters of
Edward Fitzgerald, we cannot fail to be struck
with the amount of unmixed pleasure he derived from his books, merely because he ap-
proached them with such instinctive honesty
and singleness of purpose. He was perfectly
frank in his satisfaction, and he was wholly
innocent of any didactic tendency. Those
subjects which he confessed he enjoyed be-

cause he only partly understood them, "just as the old women love sermons," he refrained from interpreting to his friends; those "large, still books," like "Clarissa Harlowe," for which he shared all Tennyson's enthusiasm, he forbore to urge upon less leisurely readers. And what a world of meaning in that single line, "For human delight, Shakespeare, Cervantes, and Scott"! For human delight! The words sound like a caress; a whole sunny vista opens before us; idleness and pleasure lure us gently on; a warm and mellow atmosphere surrounds us; we are invited, not driven, to be happy. I cannot but compare Fitzgerald reading Scott, "for human delight," in the quiet winter evenings, with a very charming old gentleman whom I recently saw working conscientiously — so I thought — through Tolstoï's "Peace and War." He sighed a little when he spoke to me, and held up the book for inspection. "My daughter-in-law sent it to me," he explained resignedly, "and said I must be sure and read it. But," — this with a sudden sense of gratitude and deliverance, — "thank Heaven! one volume was lost on the way." Now we have Mr. An-

drew Lang's word for it that the Englishmen
of to-day, "those poor islanders," indeed, are
better acquainted with "Anna Karenina" than
with "The Fortunes of Nigel," and we cannot
well doubt the assertion, in view of the too manifest regret with which it is uttered.   But then
nobody reads "The Fortunes of Nigel" because
he has been told to read it, nor because his
neighbors are reading it, nor because he wants
to say that he has read it.   The hundred and
one excellent reasons for becoming acquainted
with Tolstoï or Ibsen resolve themselves into
a single motive when we turn to Scott.   It is
"for human delight" or nothing.   And if,
even to children, this joy has grown somewhat
tasteless of late years, I fear the reason lies in
their lack of healthy unconsciousness.   They
are taught so much they did not use to know
about the correct standing of authors, they
are so elaborately directed in their recreations
as well as in their studies, that the old simple
charm of self-forgetful absorption in a book
seems well-nigh lost to them.   It is not very
encouraging to see a bright little girl of ten
making believe she enjoys Miss Austen's
novels, and to hear her mother's complacent

comments thereon, when we realize how exclusively the fine, thin perfection of Miss Austen's work appeals to the mature observation
of men and women, and how utterly out of harmony it must be with the crude judgment and
expansive ideality of a child. I am willing
to believe that these abnormally clever little
people, who read grown-up books so conspicuously in public, love their Shakespeares, and
their Grecian histories, and their " Idylls of
the King." I have seen literature of the delicately elusive order, like " The Marble Faun,"
and " Elsie Venner," and " Lamia," devoured
with a wistful eagerness that plainly revealed
the awakened imagination responding with
quick delight to the sweet and subtle charm of
mystery. But I am impelled to doubt the
attractiveness of Thackeray to the youthful
mind, even when I have just been assured that
" Henry Esmond " is " a lovely story ; " and I
am still more skeptical as to Miss Austen's
marvelous hair-strokes conveying any meaning
at all to the untrained faculties of a child.
Can it be that our boys and girls have learned
from Emerson and Carlyle not to wish to be
amused ? Or is genuine amusement so rare

that, like Mr. Payn's young friend, they have
grown reconciled to a pretended sensation, and
strive dutifully to make the most of it? Alas!
such pretenses are not always the facile things
they seem, and if a book is ever to become
a friend to either young or old, it must be
treated with that simple integrity on which all
lasting amity is built. "Read, not to con-
tradict and confute," says Lord Bacon, "nor
to believe and take for granted, nor to find
talk and discourse;" and, in the delicate
irony of this advice, we discern the satisfaction of the philosopher in having deprived the
mass of mankind of the only motives which
prompt them to read at all.

# FICTION IN THE PULPIT.

ONE of the most curious and depressing things about our modern literary criticism is the tendency it has to slide into an ethical criticism before we know what to expect. We go to a Browning Society, for example, — at least some of us who are stout-hearted go, — presumably to hear about Mr. Browning's poetry. What we do hear about are his ethics. Insinuate a doubt as to the artistic setting of a poem, and you are met at once by the spirited counter-statement that the poet has taught us a particularly noble lesson in that particularly noble verse. Push your heresy a step further by hinting that the question at issue is not so much the nobility of the lesson taught as the degree of beauty which has been made manifest in the teaching, and you find yourself in much the same position as that unfortunate Epicurean who strayed wantonly into the lecture-hall of Epictetus, and got philosophically crushed for his presumption. The

fiction of the day, a commonplace product for
the most part, which surely merits lighter treatment at our hands, is subjected to a similar
discipline ; and the novelist, finding his own
importance immensely increased thereby, rises
promptly to the emergency, and, with characteristic diffidence, consents to be our guide,
philosopher, and friend.   It is amusing to hear
Bishop Copleston, writing for that young and
vivacious generation who knew not the seriousness of life, remind them pointedly that
"the task of pleasing is at all times easier
than that of instructing." It is delightful
to think that there ever was a period when
people preferred to be pleased rather than
instructed.   It is refreshing to go back in
spirit to those halcyon days when poets
sang of their ladies' eyebrows rather than of
the inscrutable problems of fate, and when
Mrs. Battle relaxed herself, after a game of
whist, over that genial and unostentatious
trifle called a novel.   Fancy Mrs. Battle relaxing herself to-day over " Daniel Deronda,"
or " The Ordeal of Richard Feveril," or " The
Story of an African Farm "!

Vernon Lee, speaking by the mouth of

Marcel, that shadowy young Frenchman who is none the less unpleasant for being so indistinct, would have us believe that this incorrigible habit of applying ethical standpoints to artistic questions is merely an English idiosyncrasy, one of those " weird and exquisite moral impressions " which can be gathered only from contact with British soil. But in view of the deductions recently drawn from French and Russian fiction by an ingenious American critic, we are forced to conclude that true didacticism is an exotic of such rare and subtle excellence as frequently to be mistaken for vice. In fact, it is not its least advantageous peculiarity that a novelist may, on high moral grounds, treat of a great many subjects which he would be compelled rigorously to let alone, if he had no nobler object before him than the mere pleasure and entertainment of his readers. There are no improper novels any longer, because even those that strike the uninitiated as admirably adapted to the spiritual requirements of Commodus or Elagabalus are, in truth, far more moral than morality itself, being set up, like the festering heads of old-time criminals, as a

stern warning in the market-place. Zola, we
all know, aspires as much to be a teacher as
George Eliot. His methods are different,
to be sure, but the directing principle is the
same. He can neither amuse nor please, but
he can and will instruct. " When I have once
shown you," he seems to say, " every known
detail of every known sin, — and the list, it
must be confessed, is a long one, — you will
then be glad to walk purely on your appointed
path. You will remember what I have de-
scribed to you, and be cautious." But it may
fairly be doubted whether the Spartan boys,
whose anxious fathers exhibited to them the
drunken Helots sprawling swine-like in the
sun, were quite as deeply shocked at the
sight as classical history would give us to
understand. There are some old-fashioned
lines by an old-fashioned poet to the effect
that the ugliness of Vice is no especial detriment to her seductions, if we will only look
at her often enough to forget it. Probably
those Spartan lads, after a few educational
experiments, began to think that the Helots,
in their reeking filth and bestiality, were
rather interesting studies; were experiencing

new and perhaps pleasurable emotions; were more comfortable, at 'all events, than they themselves, sitting stiff and upright at the public table, with a scanty plateful of unpalatable broth; were, in short, having a jolly good time of it, — and why not try for once what such thorough-going drunkenness was like?

This point of view, however, is far too shallow and frivolous to find favor with the serious apostles who are regenerating the world by the simple process of calling old and evil things by new and beautiful names. In the days of our great-grandfathers, a novel was simply a novel. Ten chances to one it was not as virtuous as it should have been, in which case the great-grandfathers laughed over it jovially, if they chanced to be light-minded, or shook their heads impressively, if they were disposed to be grave; perhaps even going so far as to lock it up, having previously satisfied their own curiosity, from their equally curious families. But it never occurred to them to make a merit of reading "Tom Jones" or "Humphry Clinker," any more than it occurred to the authors of those ingenious books to pose as illustrative moral-

ists before the world. The men of that robust generation were better able to bear the
theory of their amusements, and vices were
quite content to flourish shamelessly under
their proper names. Cruelty then took the
form of pastime, — bear-baiting, badger-draw-
ing, cock-fighting; questionable pleasures,
doubtless, yet gentle as the sports of cherubs
when compared with the ever-increasing agonies of vivisection, with the ceaseless and
nameless experiments of German and Italian
scientists, the " Fisiologia del Dolore " of Professor Mantegazza, all of which horrors are
justified and turned into painful duties by our
new evolutionary morality. Sensuality, too,
which used to show itself coarse, smiling, un-
masked, and unmistakable, is now serious,
analytic, and so burdened with a sense of its
responsibilities that it passes muster half the
time as a new type of asceticism. The moral
animus with which Frenchmen write immoral
books is one of the paradoxes of our present
system of ethics ; and it occasionally happens
that the simple-minded reader, failing to appreciate the shadowy elevation of their platform, fancies they are working *con amore*

amid their unpromising and unsavory ma-
terials. So it was that Mr. Howells startled
a great many respectable people by the assurance that "Madame Bovary" was "one
impassioned cry of the austerest morality,"
when they had innocently supposed it to be
something vastly different. Even respectable
critics, unemancipated English critics in particular, seem to have been somewhat taken
back by the breadth of this definition. Perhaps they recalled Epictetus, — "Austerity
should be both cleanly and pleasing," — and
considered that "Madame Bovary" was neither. Perhaps they thought, and with some
reason, that never, since Swift's angry eyes
were closed in death, has any writer expressed
more harsh and cruel scorn for his fellow-men
than Gustave Flaubert, and that concentrated
contempt is seldom the most effective weapon
for an apostle. Perhaps they were merely
conventional enough to fancy that a novel,
against which even wicked Paris protested,
was hardly decorous enough for sober London. At all events, it would appear as though
a goodly number of stragglers along the path
of virtue felt themselves insufficiently advanced

for such a difficult and abstruse text-book of ethics.

In the midst of this universal disclaimer, it never seems to occur to anybody to ask the simple question, Why should " Madame Bo-vary " be an impassioned cry of the austerest morality, — why should any novel undertake to be an impassioned cry of morality at all? It is not the office of a novelist to show us how to behave ourselves; it is not the business of fiction to teach us anything. Scientific truths, new forms of religion, the humorous eccentri-cities of socialism, the countless fads of radical reformers, the proper way to live our own lives, — these matters, which are now objects of such tender regard to the story-teller, form no part of his rightful stock-in-trade. His task is simply to give us pleasure, and his duty is to give it within the not very Puritan-ical limits prescribed by our modern notions of decency. If he chooses to overstep these limits, an offense against propriety, it is exas-perating to have him defended on the score of an ethical purpose, an offense against art; for there is nothing so hopelessly inartistic as to represent the world as worse than it is, or to

express a too vehement dissatisfaction with the
men who dwell in it. Art is never didactic,
does not take kindly to facts, is helpless to
grapple with theories, and is killed outright by
a sermon. Its knowledge is not that of a
schoolmaster, and is not imparted through the
severe medium of lessons. It assumes no responsibilities, undertakes no reformation, and,
as George Sand neatly points out, proves nothing. What are we to learn, she asks, from
" Paul and Virginia " ? Merely that youth,
friendship, love, and the tropics are beautiful
things when St. Pierre describes them. What
from " Faust? " Only that science, human
life, fantastic images, profound, graceful, or
terrible ideas, are wonderful things when Goethe makes out of them a sublime and moving
picture. This sounds like high authority for
Mr. Oscar Wilde's latest and most amusing
heresy, that Nature gains her true distinction
from being reproduced, with necessary modifi-
cations, by Art ; that too close a copy of the
original is fatal to the perfection of the younger
and fairer sister ; that the insignificant and
sordid types in which Nature takes such repre-
hensible delight are to be, if possible, forgot-

ten, rather than dandled into insulting prominence ; and that not all the dreary vices of
the most drearily vicious man or woman whom
Zola ever drew can give that man or woman
a right to breathe in the tranquil air of fiction.
As for accepting inartistic and repellent sinners for the sake of the moral lesson which
may, or may not, be drawn from their sin, Mr.
Wilde is as prompt as De Quincey himself to
repudiate any such utilitarian theory. "If
you insist on my telling you what is the moral
of the Iliad," says De Quincey, "I must insist
on your telling me what is the moral of a rat-
tlesnake, or the moral of Niagara. I suppose
the moral is, that you must get out of their
way if you mean to moralize much longer."

But this light-hearted flippancy on the part
of the critic was only possible, or at least was
only acceptable, in those days when the novelist had not yet awakened to his serious
duties in life. Content, for the most part, to
tell a story, he barely remembered now and
then, in the beginning, may be, or at the end,
that there was such a thing as an ethical
purpose in·existence. Even Richardson, the
father of English didactic fiction, was but an

indifferent parent, starting out with a great
many gallant promises on behalf of his off-
spring, and easily forgetting all about them.
Miss Burney was as cheerfully unconscious of
her own grave obligations to society as was
Miss Austen ; while in those few lines with
which Sir Walter Scott closes " The Heart
of Mid - Lothian " — lines addressed to the
" reader," and containing some irrefutable but
not very original remarks about the happiness
of virtue and the infelicity of vice — we see an
almost pathetic avowal on the part of the great
novelist that, in the mere delight of telling his
beautiful and best loved tale, he had well-
nigh lost sight of any moral lesson it might
be fitted to convey, and was trying at the last
moment to make amends for this deficiency.
Imagine George Eliot forgetting, or permit-
ting her readers to forget, the moral lesson of
" Adam Bede," when every fresh development
of character or of narrative has for its conscious purpose the driving home of hard and
bitter truths. No need for the authoress of
" Romola " to wind up her story with that
paragraph of excellent advice to poor little
Lillo, who is after all rather young to profit

by it ; while we who have followed Tito from
his first joyous entrance into Florence to that
last dreadful moment when, floating, bruised,
beautiful, and helpless, down the Arno, he
opens his dying eyes to meet the horror of
Baldassarre's vengeance, — we surely do not
require to be warned afresh against the unpar-
donable sin of making things easy for ourselves. In the pathetic history of the marred
and broken lives of " Middlemarch," in the
darker and harsher tragedy of " Daniel Deronda," we see forever present upon each succeeding page the underlying motive of the
tale ; we hear George Eliot listening, as Mor-
ley says, to the sound of her own voice, and
announcing as distinctly as she announced in
life that her function is that of the æsthetic
teacher, to rouse the nobler emotions which
make mankind desire the social right.

If the test of the true artist be to conceal
his art, then this transparently didactic purpose is fatal to the perfection of any work
claiming to spring from the imagination. It
is impossible to preach a sermon out of the
mouth of fiction without making the fiction
subordinate to the sermon, and thus at once

destroying the just proportions of a story, and
forfeiting that subtle sympathy with life, as it
is, which gives to every artistic masterpiece its
admirable air of self-sufficing and harmonious
repose. " I always tremble when I see a
philosophical idea attached to a novel," said
Sainte-Beuve, who was spared by the kindly
hand of death from the sight of countless
novels attached to philosophical ideas. Charles
Lamb, with that unerring intuition which was
the most wonderful thing about his indolent
luminous genius, recognized, even in the comparative sunlight of his day, the growing
shadow of a speculative, disciplinal, analytic
literature which should sadly overrate its own
responsibilities and importance. " We turn
away," he said, " from the real essences of
things to hunt after their relative shadows,
moral duties ; whereas, if the truth of things
were fairly represented, the relative duties
might be safely trusted to themselves, and
moral philosophy lose the name of a science."
No one understood more thoroughly than
Lamb that the purely natural point of view,
as apart from the purely ethical point of view,
supplies the proper basis for all imaginative

writing. " I have lived to grow into an in-
decent character," he sighed, struggling with
whimsical dejection to comprehend the new
forces at work ; sometimes protesting angrily
against the " Puritanical obtuseness, the stupid,
infantile goodness which is creeping among
us, instead of the vigorous passions and virtues clad in flesh and blood ; " sometimes contemplating, with humorously lowered eyelids,
" the least little men who spend their time and
lose their wits in chasing nimble and retiring
Truth, to the extreme perturbation and drying
up of the moistures."

> " On court, hélas ! après la vérité ;
> Ah ! croyez-moi, l'erreur a son mérite."

But if modern novelists are disposed to sacrifice their art to a conscious ethical purpose,
to write fiction, as Mr. Oscar Wilde wittily
says, " as though it were a painful duty," it
can hardly be denied that they are giving the
public what the public craves ; that they are
on the safe side of criticism, and have chosen
their position wisely, if not well. Should any
one feel inclined to doubt this, it might be
a convincing and salutary exercise to re-read
as swiftly as possible a few of the numerous

essays and reviews which followed closely on
George Eliot's death, and which have not
altogether vanished from the literary market
now. With one or two distinct and admirable exceptions, they deal almost exclusively
with the didactic aspect of her novels; they
weigh and balance every social theory, every
spiritual problem, every moral lesson, to be
extracted from her pages; they take her as
seriously as she took herself, and give their
keenest praise to those precise qualities which
marred the artistic perfection of her work. I
have myself counted the obnoxious word "ethics" six times repeated in the opening paragraph of one review, and have felt too deeply
disheartened by such an outset to penetrate
any further. On the other hand, her dramatic power, her subtle insight, her masterly
style, her warm and vivid pictures of a life
that has touched us so closely, the exquisite
art with which her earlier tales are con-
structed, and, above and beyond all, her
delicious and inimitable humor, — these things
appear to be regarded as mere minor details,
useful perhaps and pleasing, but strictly subordinate to the nobler endowments of her

spirit. That some of us endure George Eliot the teacher for the sake of George Eliot the story-teller is a truth too painful to be put often into words. That little Maggie Tulliver spelling out the examples in the Latin grammar, and secretly delighted at her own amazing cleverness, enables some of us to support the processional virtues of Romola, and the deadly priggishness of Daniel Deronda, is a melancholy fact which perhaps it would be wiser to ignore. Maggie, as we are aware, has deeply shocked the sensitive nature of Mr. Swinburne by her grossness in falling in love with Stephen, for no better reason, apparently, than because he was the first big, and strong, and handsome man she had ever known. That wonderful scene on the boat, with its commonplace setting and strained intensity of emotion; the short, sad, rapturous flight; the few misty hours of passionate dreaming which made poor Maggie's little share of earthly happiness, have branded her so deeply in the sight of this hardened moralist that even her bitter agony of renunciation and her final triumph have failed to win her pardon. With what chastened severity

and with what an animated vocabulary he
condemns the " revolting avowal " of her love,
the "hideous transformation," the " vulgar
and brutal outrage," the "radical and moral
plague spot," which debases her into something
too vile for pity or redemption ! Verily, this
is the squeamishness of the true ascetic who
has somehow mistaken his vocation, and there
will be a scant allowance of cakes and ale for
any of us when it is Mr. Swinburne's turn to
be virtuous.

As for the humor of George Eliot's novels,
that mysterious humor which she herself was
not humorous enough to appreciate, it de-
serves better treatment at our hands, were
it only for the sake of its valuable adapta-
bility, were it only because it is pliant enough
to fit in all the time with our own duller
imaginings, and to afford a basis and an illustration for our own inadequate thoughts.
From what depths of her sombre nature came
those arrow - points tipped with fire, or,
choicer still, those tempered shafts of reflective ridicule, which are kindly enough to
win our unhesitating acquiescence ? With
what pleasure we are reminded that " people

who live at a distance are naturally less faulty than those immediately under our own eyes, and it seems superfluous, when we consider the geographical position of the Ethiopians, and how very little the Greeks had to do with them, to inquire further why Homer calls them 'blameless' "! Surely, to express a truth humorously is to rob that truth of all offensive qualities, and Lucian himself would be prepared to admit that, in a case like this, it is almost as pleasant as falsehood. But to beguile us into the grateful shades of fiction, as Jael beguiled Sisera into the shelter of her tent, and then, with deadly purpose, to transfix us with a truth as sharp and cruel as the nail with which Jael slew her guest, is a dastardly betrayal of confidence. When a novelist undertakes to sit in judgment upon his characters, for the sake of illustrating some moral lesson with which he has no need to concern himself, he rudely breaks the mystic web of illusion, and destroys the charm which binds us to his side. What is it that gives to "Henry Esmond" its supreme artistic value, if not the fact that Thackeray sank himself out of sight; was content for once to look at

things with Esmond's gentle eyes, to judge of
things with Esmond's tolerant soul; and forbore to whip his actors through the play like
criminals at the cart-tail? On the other
hand, what whimsical sense of responsibility
induced Bulwer to elaborate a character like
Randal Leslie, only to make of him an educational sign-post, after the approved fashion of
Miss Edgeworth's "Early Lessons"? Judged
by a purely ethical standard, Randal no doubt
merited his failure; judged by the standard
of his ability and energy, Reynard the Fox was
as little likely to fail; and though Mr. Froude
tells us that "women, with their clear moral
insight, have no sympathy with Reynard's
successful villainy," yet I doubt whether we
should really like to see him outwitted by a
fool like Bruin, or beaten by a bully like Ise-
grim. He is a terrible scamp, to be sure, but
the charm of the situation is that we are not
compelled to watch it from a jury-box.

Now the disadvantage of being at once a
novelist and a teacher is that you have no
neutral ground from which to observe your
characters, no friendly appreciation of things
or people as you find them. What the ar-

tist accepts with delicate sympathy, though
with no pretense at justification, the moralist
must either justify or condemn. The first
course is common enough, and produces a
class of literature essentially vicious because
of its very limitations, — six deadly sins held
up to public execration, and the seventh presented to us tenderly as an ill-understood and
sadly calumniated virtue. The second course
—that of implied condemnation — is equally
open to a Sunday-school story or to the least
decorous of French novels; both have for
their avowed object the pillorying of vice, and
both put forward this claim as a reasonable
excuse for existence. But art has no pillory,
no stocks, no whipping-post, no exclusive
methods for fixing our attention upon sin.
Art gives us Lady Macbeth and Iago, and
gives them to us without reproaches, without
extenuation, and without any attempt to re-
form. It is less painful to watch the irresistible development of their respective crimes
than to hear Thackeray lashing with keen
scorn some poor sinner stumbling through the
mazes of worldly wickedness, or to see George
Eliot pursuing one of her own creations

with inextinguishable severity and contempt.
There is something paralyzing in the cold
anger with which Rosamond Vincy is branded
and shamed; there is something appalling in
the conscientious vindictiveness with which
Tito is hunted down, step by step, to his final
retribution.    That  delightful  essayist, Mr.
Karl Hillebrand, whose artistic nature is
about as much at home among modern theories as a strayed Faun in a button factory,
has given us a half-humorous, half-despairing
picture of some old acquaintances under the
new dispensation: of Manon Lescaut threatened with Charlotte Brontë's birch-rod; of
Squire Western opening his startled eyes as
Zola proceeds to detail for his benefit the
latest and most highly realistic study of de-
lirium tremens; of Falstaff, whom that losel
Shakespeare treated so indulgently, listening
abashed to George Eliot's scathing denuncia-
tions.  " For really, Sir John," he hears her
say, " you have no excuse whatever.  If you
were a poor devil who had never had any
but bad examples before your eyes! — but
you have had all the advantages which destiny can give to man on his way through life.

Are you not born of a good family? Have
you not had at Oxford the best education
England is able to give to her children?
Have you not had the highest connections?
And, nevertheless, how low you have fallen!
Do you know why? I have warned my Tito
over and over again against it: because you
have always done that only which was agreeable to you, and have shunned everything that
was unpleasant."

This sounds like sad trifling to our sober
and orthodox ears, but it is not more audacious, on the whole, than the pathetic lamenta-
tions of Mr. Oscar Wilde over the career of
Charles Reade: the most disheartening, he
protests, in all literature; "wasted in a foolish attempt to be modern, and to draw attention to the state of our convict prisons, and
the management of private lunatic asylums.
Charles Dickens was depressing enough, in all
conscience, when he tried to arouse our sympathy for the victims of the poor-law administration; but Charles Reade, an artist, a scholar,
a man with a true sense of beauty, raging
and roaring over the abuses of modern life
like a common pamphleteer or a sensational

journalist, is really a sight for the angels to weep over." It is just possible that whatever personal interest the angelic hosts take in our earthly lot may be directed to philanthropy rather than to literature ; but, for the idle and inglorious mortal, the protest holds a world of truth and meaning. Reade, as a reformer, is melancholy company ; and Dickens is inexpressibly dismal when he drags the Chancery business into " Bleak House," and the pauper dinner-table into " Oliver Twist," and that dreary caricature, the Circumlocution Office, into " Little Dorrit." If these things really accomplished the good that is claimed for them, it was dearly bought by the weariness of so many millions of readers. " A fiction contrived to support an opinion is a vicious composition," said Jeffrey, who was as apt in his general criticisms as he was awkward in their particular applications, and who lived before the era of serious and educational novels. To-day we have the unhesitating assertion of Mr. Howells that one of Tolstoï's highest claims to our consideration is his steadfast teaching " that all war, private and public, is a sin." Mr. Ruskin, it may be remembered, holds some-

what different views: "There is no great art
possible to a nation but that which is based
on war." Yet as every man is entitled to his
own opinion in such matters, there is no reason
why we should quarrel with either the Russian
or the Englishman for their chosen principles.
But Ruskin is no greater as an essayist because he approves of war, and Tolstoï gains
nothing as a novelist because he adheres to
peace. The glory of the battlefield, its pathos
and its horror, are all fitting subjects for the
artist's pen or pencil. He may stir our blood
and rouse our fighting instincts, like Homer or
Scott; or he may move us to pity, and sorrow,
and shame, by the revelation of all the shat-
tered hopes and bitter agonies that lie beyond.
But his own greatness depends exclusively on
his treatment of the subject, and not on his
point of view. Who knows and who cares
what De Neuville thinks of war? He paints
for us a handful of men roused at dawn, and
rushing gallantly to their deaths, and we feel
our hearts beat high as we look at them. The
terror, the awfulness, the self-forgetting courage, the gay defiance of battle, all are there,
imprisoned mysteriously in the artistic group-

ing of a few blue-coated soldiers. But Vere-
stchagin, who aspires to teach us the wickedness of war, is powerless to thrill us in this
manner. He is probably sincere in his opinions,
and he has striven hard to give them form and
expression, but, lacking the artistic impulse,
he has for the most part striven in vain. His
huge canvases, packed with dead and dying,
are less impressive, less solemn, less painful
even, from their monotonous overcrowding,
than a single Zouave, whose wounds De Neuville has no need to emphasize with vast expenditure of vermilion, when the faintness of
a mortal agony draws his weary body to the
earth. " All real power," says Ruskin, " lies
in delicacy." To trouble the senses is an easy
task, but it is through the imagination only
that we receive any strong and lasting impressions, and no sincerity of purpose can suffice
to turn a crude didacticism into art.

It is hard to analyze the peculiar nature of
the claims asserted and upheld by the disciples
of modern realism. They are not content
with the splendid position which is theirs by
right, — not content with the admirable work
they have done, and the hold they have se-

cured on the sympathies of our earnest, ration-
alistic, and unimaginative age; but they assume in some subtle and incomprehensible
way that their school is based upon man's
love and appreciation for his fellow-creatures.
If we would but look upon all men as our
brothers, it is plainly hinted, all men would be
of equal interest to us, and it is our duty, as
nineteenth-century citizens, to accept and cherish this universal relationship.  To the perpetual sounding of the humanitarian note, there
are some, it is true, who answer, with Vernon
Lee's very amusing and very wicked skeptic,
that " the new-fangled bore called mankind is
as great a plague as the old-fashioned nuisance
called a soul; " but there are others who, finding themselves in full possession of a conscience, stoutly maintain that they love their
undistinguished brother none the less because
they weary of his society in literature and art.
It was Ruskin, for example, who sneered at
George Eliot's characters as the " sweepings of
a Pentonville omnibus," — a terrible misap-
plication of an inspired phrase; but Ruskin
is the last man in Christendom who can be
accused of an indifference to his fellow-men.

His whole life is a sufficient refutation of the charge. Voltaire is responsible for the statement that the world is full of people who are not worth knowing. Yet Voltaire was forever restlessly espousing some popular cause, forever interesting himself in the supposed welfare of these eminently undesirable associates. What he thought, and what he was quite right in thinking, is that we gain nothing, intellectually or spiritually, from the mass of men and women with whom we come in contact; and that it is wiser to fix our attention upon graceful and exalted types than to go on forever, as Charles Lamb expressed it, "encouraging each other in mediocrity."

The present stand of realism, however, is but one more phase of the intrusion of ethics upon art, — the assumption that I cannot have a sincere regard for the welfare of my washerwoman if I do not care for her company either in a book or out of it. Tubs have grown in favor since the day when Wordsworth was compelled, " in deference to the opinion of friends," to substitute an impossible turtle-shell for the homely vessel in which the blind Highland boy set sail on Loch Leven. All

classes and all people, I am now given to understand, are of supreme interest to the loving
student of human nature, and it is a " narrow
conservatism " — chilling phrase — that seeks
to limit the artist's field of action. But as
limiting the artist's field of action is practically
impossible, and not often essayed, it is hard to
understand what the respective schools of fiction find to fight over, and why this new battle
of the books should be raging as fiercely as if
there were any visible cause of war. It is not
an orderly and well-appointed battle, either,
confined to the ranks of critics and reviewers,
but a free skirmish, where everybody who has
written a novel rushes in and plays an active
part. Conflicting opinions rattle around our
heads like hail, and the voice of the peace-
maker, — Mr. Andrew Lang, — protesting that
all schools are equally good, if the scholars
are equal to their tasks, is lost in the universal clamor. The only point on which any two
sharpshooters appear to agree is in laying the
blame for the " unmanly timidity of English
fiction " — a timidity not always so apparent
as it might be — on the shoulders of women,
who, it seems, will have all novels modeled to

suit themselves, and who, with the arrogance of supreme power, have réversed the political situation, and deprived mankiṇd of their vote. This is the opinion of Rider Haggard, and also of Vernon Lee, who asserts that "the ethics of fiction are framed entirely for the benefit or the detriment of women," and that its enforced morality — a defect which, to do her justice, she is striving her best to eradicate — is fatal to its mission in life.

But that fiction has a mission, nobody dares to doubt; that its ethics are of paramount importance, nobody dares to deny. It devotes itself in all seriousness to our moral and intellectual welfare; and if, now and then, we are reminded of Sydney Smith, who would rather Mr. Perceval had whipped his boys and saved his country, we stifle the sinful impulse, and turn to biography and history for recreation, for that purely imaginative element which places no tax upon our conscience or credulity. Yet we may at least remember that all natures do not develop on the same lines; that all goodness is not comprised within certain recognized virtues, or limited to certain fields of thought. Tolstoï, a figure on a grand scale, "filled with pity for the oppressed, the poor, and the lowly," has manifested the sincerity of his creed by a life of hard work and hearty renunciation. But Sir Walter Scott, the Tory, the "feudalist," content to take the world as he found it, and to believe that whatever is, is right, proved himself no less the friend and benefactor of his kind. The halo round his head is not that of genius only, but of love, — love freely given and abundantly returned. The anxious whisper of the London workmen to Allan Cunningham, "Do you know, sir, if this is the street where *he* is lying?" the rapturous cry of the little deformed tailor who, with his last breath, sobbed out, "The Lord bless and reward you!" and, falling back, expired, — these are the sounds that ring through generations to bear witness to man's fidelity to man.

> "For the might
> Of the whole world's good wishes with him goes,"

sang Wordsworth, with whom affectionate hyperbole was hardly a common fault. It cannot be that Mr. Howells believes in his heart that American children need to be warned against Sir Walter's errors, and that it is the duty of American parents to give this solemn warning. Consider that it is only in youth that our imagination triumphs vividly over realities, — a triumph short-lived enough, but rich in fruits for the future. The time comes all too soon when we doubt, and question, and make room in our puzzled minds for the opinions of many men. Ah, leave to the child, at least, his clear, intuitive, unbiased enjoyment, his sympathy with things that have been! He is not so easily hurt as we suppose; he is strong in his elastic ignorance, and has no need of a pepsin pill with every mouthful of literary food he swallows. Mental hygiene, it is said, is apt to lead to mental valetudinarianism; but if we are to turn our very nurseries into hot-beds of prigs, we may say once more what was said when Chapelain published his portentous epic, that "a new horror has been added to the accomplishment of reading."

# PLEASURE : A HERESY.

IT is an interesting circumstance in the lives of those persons who are called either heretics or reformers, according to the mental attitudes or antecedent prejudices of their critics, that they always begin by hinting their views with equal modesty and moderation. It is only when rubbed sore by friction, when hard driven and half spent, that they venture into the open, and define their positions before the world in all their bald malignity. Now I have a certain sneaking sympathy, not with heretics or reformers, either, but with that frame of mind which compels a hunted and harried creature suddenly to assume the offensive, cast prudence to the winds, nail his thesis conspicuously to the doorpost, and snortingly await developments. He is not, while so occupied, a winning or beautiful figure, when judged by the strict standards of sweetness and light; but he is eminently human, and is entitled to the forbearance of humanity.

It is now over a year since, in an article
called " Fiction in the Pulpit," and published
in the " Atlantic Monthly," I ventured to say,
or rather I said without any consciousness of
being venturesome, that the sole business of
a novel-writer was to give us pleasure; his '
sole duty was to give it to us within decent
and prescribed limits. It seemed to me then
that the assertion was so self-evident as to be
hardly worth the making; it was a little like
saying an undisputed thing " in such a solemn
way." I have learned since how profoundly
I was mistaken in the temper, not of writers
only, but of readers as well, — how far remote I stood from the current of ethical
activity. It is needless to state that this later
knowledge has been brought to me by the
mouths of critics : sometimes by professional
critics, who said their say in print ; sometimes
by amateur and neighborly critics, who expressed theirs frankly in speech. It is needless, also, to state that, of the two, the professional critics — brothers and sisters of my
own household I count them — have been
infinitely more tolerant of my shortcomings,
more lenient in their remonstrances, more per-

suasive and even flattering in their lines of
argument. The ordinary reviewer, anony-
mous or otherwise, is not the ruthless de-
stroyer, " ferocious, dishonest, butcherly,"
whom Mr. Howells so graphically portrays,
but rather a kindly, indifferent sort of creature, who cares so little what you think that
even his reproaches wear an air of gentle and
friendly unconcern.

In all cases, however, the verdict reached
was practically the same. The business of
fiction is to elevate our moral tone; to teach
us the stern lessons of life; to quicken our
conceptions of duty; to show us the dark
abysses of fallen nature; to broaden our
spiritual vistas; to destroy our old comfortable creeds; to open our half-closed eyes; to
expand our souls with the generous sentiments of humanity; to vex us with social
problems and psychological conundrums; to
gird us with chain armor for our daily battles; to do anything or everything, in short,
except simply give us pleasure. It is not
forbidden us, to be sure, to take delight, if
we can, in the system of instruction; a good
child, we are told, should always love its les-

sons; but the really important thing is to
study and know them by heart. Verily

"This rugged virtue makes me gasp"!

Why should the word " pleasure," when used
in connection with literature, send a cold
chill down our strenuous nineteenth-century
spines? It is a good and charming word,
caressing in sound and softly exhilarating in
sense. As in a dream, it shows us swiftly
rich minutes by a winter firelight, with " The
Eve of St. Agnes " held in our happy hands ;
long, lazy summer afternoons spent right joyously in company with Emma Woodhouse and
Mr. Knightley ; or, perhaps, hours of content,
lost in the letters of Charles Lamb, dear to
us alike in all seasons and in all moods, a
heritage of delight as long as life shall last.
I do not, indeed, as I have been accused of
doing, employ the word " pleasure " as synonymous with amusement. Amusement is merely
one side of pleasure, but a very excellent
side, against which, in truth, I have no evil
word to urge. The gods forbid such base and
savorless ingratitude ! This is not at best a
merry world. " There is a certain grief in

things as they are, in man as he has come to be;" and the background of our lives is a steady, undeviating sadness. Who, then, has not felt that sudden lifting of the spirits, that quick purging of black, melancholy vapors from the brain, as wise old Burton would express it, when some fine jest appeals irresistibly to one's sense of humor! There comes to the alert mind at such a moment a distinct revelation of contentment; a conscious thought that it is well to be alive, and to hear that nimble witticism which has so warmed and tickled one's fancy. "Live merrily as thou canst," says Burton, "for by honest mirth we cure many passions of the mind. A gay companion is as a wagon to him that is wearied by the way."

If amusement can help us so materially in our daily life, which is a daily struggle as well, how much more pleasure! — pleasure which is the rightful goal of art, just as knowledge is the rightful goal of science. "Art," says Winckelmann, "is the daughter of Pleasure;" and as Demeter sought for Persephone with resistless fervor and desire, so Pleasure seeks for Art, languishing in sunless gloom, and, having found her, expresses through her the joy and beauty of existence, and lives again herself in the possession of her fair child, while the whole earth bubbles into laughter. We cannot separate these two without exchanging sunlight for frost and the cold, dark winter nights. Mr. E. S. Dallas, who, in those charming volumes pleadingly entitled " The Gay Science," has made a gallant fight for pleasure as the end of art, and for criticism as the path by which that end is reached, shows us very clearly and very persuasively that, in all ages and in all nations, there has been a natural, wholesome, outspoken conviction that art exists for pleasure, and, pleasing, instructs as well. There is a core of truth, he grants, in the Horatian maxim that art may be profitable as well as delightful, " since it always holds that wisdom's ways are ways of pleasantness, that enduring pleasure comes only out of healthful action, and that amusement, as mere amusement, is in its own place good if it be but innocent. There is profit in art, as there is gain in godliness, and policy in an honest life. But we are not to pursue art for profit, nor godliness for gain, nor honesty because it is politic."

This, then, is the earliest lesson that the student of art has to learn : that it exists for pleasure, but for a pleasure that may be profitable, and that stands in no sort of opposition to truth. " Science," says Mr. Dallas, " gives us truth without reference to pleasure, but immediately and chiefly for the sake of knowledge. Art gives us truth without reference to knowledge, but immediately and mainly for the sake of pleasure." The test of science, then, must always be an increase of knowledge, of proven and demonstrable facts ; the test of art must always be an increase of pleasure, of conscious and sentient joy. " What is good only because it pleases," says Dr. Johnson, " cannot be pronounced good until it has been found to please."

The joy that is born of art is not always a simple or easily analyzed emotion. The pleasure we take in looking at the soft, white, dimpled Venus of the Capitol is something very different from that strange tugging at our heart-strings when we first see the sad and scornful beauty of the Venus of Milo, or

the curious pity with which we watch the
dejected Cupid of the Vatican hanging his
lovely head. But with both the Venus of
Milo and the Vatican Cupid, the sensation of
pleasure they afford is greater than the sensation of pain, or pity, or regret. It triumphs
wholly over our other emotions, and gains
fullness from the conflict of our thoughts.
We feel many things, but we feel pleasure
most of all, and this is the final test and the
final victory of art. In the same manner, the
mixed emotions with which we listen to music
resolve themselves ultimately to pleasure in
that music; and the mixed emotions with
which we read poetry resolve themselves ultimately to pleasure in that poetry. If it were
otherwise, we should know that the music and
the poetry had failed in their crucial trial. If
we did not feel more pleasure than pain in the
tragedy of " Othello," it would not be a great
play. That we do feel more pleasure than
pain, that our pleasure is subtly fed by our
pain, proves it to be a masterpiece of art.

There is still another point to urge. While
art may instruct as well as please, it can nevertheless be true art without instructing, but

not without pleasing. The former quality is accidental, the latter essential, to its being. " Enjoyment," says Schiller, " may be only a subordinate object in life; it is the highest in art." We cannot say that " The Eve of St. Agnes " teaches us, directly or indirectly, anything whatever. The trembling lovers, the withered Angela, the revelers,

" The carved angels, ever eager-eyed,"

the storm without, the fragrant warmth and light within, are all equally innocent of moral emphasis. Even the Beadsman is not worked up, as he might have been, into a didactic agent. But every beauty-laden line is rich in pleasure, the whole poem is an inheritance of delight. I never read it without being reminded afresh of that remonstrance offered so gently by Keats to Shelley, — by Keats, who was content to be a poet, to Shelley, who would also be a reformer : " You will, I am sure, forgive me for sincerely remarking that you might curb your magnanimity, and be more of an artist, and load every rift of your subject with ore." Load every rift of your subject with ore, — there spoke the man who claimed no more for himself than that he had loved "the principle of beauty in all things," and to whose hushed and listening soul the cry of Shelley's "divine discontent" rang jarringly in the stillness of the night. If the poetry of Keats, a handful of scattered jewels left us by a dying boy, is, as Matthew Arnold admits, more solid and complete than Shelley's superb and piercing song, to what is this due, save that Keats possessed, in addition to his poetic gift, the tranquil artist soul; content, as Goethe was content, to love the principle of beauty, and to be in sympathy with the great living past which has nourished, and still nourishes, the living present. The passion for reconstructing society, and for distributing pamphlets as a first step in the reconstruction, had no part in his artistic development. The errors of his fellow-mortals touched him lightly; their superstitions did not trouble him at all; their civil rights and inherited diseases were not matters of daily thought and analysis. But what he had to give them he gave unstintedly, and we to-day are rich in the fullness of his gift. "The proper and immediate object

of poetry," says Coleridge, "is the commu-
nication of immediate pleasure; " and are our
lives so joyous that this boon may go un-
recognized and unregarded? Which is best
for us in this chilly world, — that which
pleases, but does not instruct, like "The Eve
of St. Agnes," or that which instructs, but does
not please, like Dr. Ibsen's "Ghosts"? I do
not say, which is true art? because the relative positions of the two authors forbid comparison; but, judged by the needs of humanity, which is the finer gift to earth? If, with
Pliny, we seek an escape from mortality in
literature, which shall be our choice? If, with
Dr. Johnson, we require that a book should
help us either to enjoy life or to endure it,
which shall we take for a friend?

"Everything that is any way beautiful is
beautiful in itself, and terminates in itself,"
says Marcus Aurelius; and the pleasure we
derive from a possession of beauty has characteristic completeness and vitality. This
pleasure is not only, as we are so often told,
a temporary escape from pain; it is not a
negation, a mere cessation of suffering; it is
not necessarily preceded by craving or fol-

lowed by satiety; it is emphatically not a matter of prospect as Shelley would have us believe;[1] it is a matter of conscious possession. "Vivre, c'est penser et sentir son âme;" and when a happy moment, complete and rounded as a pearl, falls into the tossing ocean of life, it is never wholly lost. For our days are made up of moments and our years of days, and every swift realization of a lawful joy is a distinct and lasting gain in our onward flight to eternity.

It seems to me strangely cruel that this philosophy of pleasure should be so ruthlessly at variance with the ethical criticism of our day. If it has come down to us as a gracious gift from the most cheerful and not the least wholesome of heathens, it has been broadened and brightened into fresh comeliness by the spirit of Christianity, which is, above all things, a spirit of lawful and recognized joy. Nothing is more plain to us in the teaching of the early Church than that asceticism is for the chosen few, and enjoyment, diffused, genial, temperate, and pure enjoyment, is for the

[1] "Pain or pleasure, if subtly analyzed, will be found to consist entirely in prospect."

many. "Put on, therefore, gladness that hath always favor with God, and is acceptable unto him, and delight thyself in it; for every man that is glad doeth the things that are good, and thinketh good thoughts, despising grief."[1] Through all the centuries, rational Christianity has still taught us bravely to endure what we must, and gratefully to enjoy what we can. There is a very charming and sensible letter on this point, written by the Abbé Duval to Madame de Rémusat, who was disposed to reproach herself a little for her own happiness, and to think that she had no right to be so comfortable and so well content.

"You say that you are happy," writes this gentlest and wisest of confessors; "why then distress yourself? Your happiness is a proof of God's love toward you; and if in your heart you truly love Him, can you refuse to respond to the divine benevolence? . . . Engrave upon your conscience this fundamental truth: that religion demands order above all things; and that, since the institutions of society have been allowed and consecrated, there is encouragement for those duties by which they are

[1] *Shepherd of Hermas.*

maintained. . . . But especially banish from
your mind the error that our pains alone are acceptable to God. A general willingness to bear
trial is enough. Never fear but life and time
will bring it. Dispose yourself beforehand to
resignation, and meanwhile thank God incessantly for the peace which pervades your lot."

This is something very different from Ruskin's ethics, — from the plain statement that
we have no right to be happy while our brother
suffers, no right to put feathers in our own
child's hat, while somebody else's child goes
featherless and ragged. But there is a certain
staying power in the older and simpler doctrine,
and an admirable truth in the gentle suggestion
that we need not vex ourselves too deeply with
the notion of our ultimate freedom from trial.
It was not given to Madame de Rémusat, any
more than it is given to us, to ride in untrou-
bled gladness over a stony world. All that she
attained, all that we can hope for, are distinct
and happy moments, brief intervals from
pain, or from that rational *ennui* which is in-
separable from the conditions of human life.
But I cannot agree with the long list of philo-
sophers and critics, from Kant and Schopen-

hauer down to Mr. Dallas, who have taught
that these passing moments are negative ir
their character; that they are hidden from our
consciousness and elude our scrutiny, — exist-
ing while we are content simply to enjoy them,
vanishing, if, like Psyche, we seek to understand our joy.  The trained intelligence grasps
its pleasures, and recognizes them as such; not
after they have fled, and linger only, a golden
haze, in memory, but alertly, in the present,
while they still lie warm in the hollow of the
heart.   There is indeed a certain breathless
and unconscious delight in life itself, which is
born of our ceaseless struggle to live, a sweetness of honey snatched from the lion's mouth.
This delight is common to all men, and is
probably keenest in those who struggle hardest.
When society is reorganized on a Utopian
basis, and nobody has any further need to
elbow his own way through hardships and dif-
ficulties, there will be one joy less in the
world; and, missing it, many people will realize that all which made life worth having has
been softened and improved out of existence.
They will cease to value, and refuse to possess,
that which costs them nothing to preserve.

This fundamental happiness in life, and in the enforced activity by which it is maintained, is hidden from our consciousness. We feel the hardships, and do not especially feel any relish in ceaselessly combating them, though the relish is there; not keen enough for palpable felicity, but vital enough to keep the human race alive. All other pleasures, however, we should train ourselves to enjoy. They flow from many sources, and are fitted to many moods. They are fed alike by our most secret emotions and by our severest toil, by the simplest thing in nature and by the utmost subtlety of art. A primrose by a river's brim often makes its appeal as vainly as does Hamlet, or the Elgin Marbles. What we need is, not more cultivation, but a recognized habit of enjoyment. There is, I am told, though I cannot speak from experience, a very high degree of pleasure in successfully working out a mathematical problem. Burton confesses frankly that his impelling motive, in long hours of research, was primarily his own gratification. "The delight is it I aim at, so great pleasure, such sweet content, there is in study." I think the most beautiful figure in recent literature is Mr. Pater's Marius the Epicurean, whose life, regarded from the outside, is but a succession of imperfect results, yet who, deserted and dying, counts over with a patient and glad heart the joys he has been permitted to know.

" Like a child thinking over the toys it loves, one after another, that it may fall asleep so, and the sooner forget all about them, he would try to fix his mind, as it were impassively, on all the persons he had loved in life, — on his love for them, dead or living, grateful for his love or not, rather than on theirs for him, — letting their images pass away again, or rest with him, as they would. One after another, he suffered those faces and voices to come and go, as in some mechanical exercise; as he might have repeated all the verses he knew by heart, or like the telling of beads, one by one, with many a sleepy nod between whiles."

Here is a profound truth, delicately and reverently conveyed. That which is given us for our joy is ours as long as life shall last; not passing away with the moment of enjoyment, but dwelling with us, and enriching us to the end. The memory of a past pleasure, derived

from any lawful source, is a part of the pleasure itself, a vital part, which remains in our
keeping as long as we recognize and cherish it.
Thus, the pleasure obtained from seeing the
Venus of Milo or reading " The Eve of St. Agnes " is not ended when we have left the Louvre
or closed the book. It becomes a portion of
our inheritance, a portion of the joy of living :
and the statue and the poem have fulfilled their
allotted purpose in yielding us this delight.
There is a curious fashion nowadays of criticis-
ing art and poetry, and even fiction, with scant
reference to the pleasure for which they exist ;
yet a rational estimate of these things is hardly
possible from any other standpoint. Mr. Ruskin, we know, has invented that pleasing novelty, ethical art-criticism, and, by its means, as
Mr. Dallas frankly admits, he has made, not
the criticism only, but the art itself, intelligi-
ble and palatable to his English readers. It
would seem as if they hardly held themselves
justified in enjoying a thing unless there was
a moral meaning back of it, a moral principle
involved in their own happiness. This meaning and this principle Mr. Ruskin has supplied,
bringing to bear upon his task all the earnest-

ness and sincerity of his spirit, all the wonderful charm and beauty of a winning and persuasive eloquence. It is well-nigh impossible
to withstand his appeals, they are so irresistibly worded; and it is only when we have with-
drawn from his seductive influence, to think a
little for ourselves, that we realize how much
of his criticism, as criticism, is valueless, because it consists in analyzing motives rather
than in estimating results. He assumes that
the first interest in a picture is, what did the
painter intend? the second interest is, how did
he carry out his intention? whereas the one
really important and paramount consideration
in art is workmanship. We have, many of us,
the artist's soul, but few the artist's fingers.
It is a pleasant pastime to decipher the mental attitude of the painter; it is essential to understand the quality and limit of his powers.

Reading Mr. Ruskin's criticisms on Tinto-
ret's pictures in the Scuola di S. Rocco — on
the Annunciation particularly — is very much
like listening to a paper in a Browning Society.
Perhaps the poet, perhaps the painter, did mean
all that. It is manifestly impossible to prove
they did n't, inasmuch as death has removed

them from any chance of interrogation. But by what mysterious and exclusive insight have Mr. Ruskin and the Browning student found it out? The interpretation is not suggested as feasible, it is asserted as a fact; though precisely how it has been reached we are not suffered to know. Many unkind and severe things have been said about judicial criticism, but Mr. Ruskin's criticism is not judicial,— which infers an application of governing principles; it is dogmatic, the unhesitating expression of a personal sentiment. He shows you Giotto's frescoes in the cloister of Santa Maria Novella; he pleads with you very prettily and charmingly to admire the Birth of the Virgin; he points out to you with rather puzzling precision exactly what the painter intended to imply by every detail of the work. This is pleasant enough; but suppose you don't really care about the Birth of the Virgin when you see it; suppose you fail to follow the guiding finger that reveals to you its significance and beauty. What happens then? Mr. Ruskin retorts in the severest manner, and with a degree of scorn that seems hardly warranted by the contingency: "If you can be pleased with this, you

can see Florence. But if not, by all means
amuse yourself there, if you find it amusing,
as long as you like ; you can never see it."

So Florence with all its loveliness is lost to
you, unless you can sufficiently sympathize with
one small fresco. It would be as reasonable
to say that all English literature is lost to you,
unless you truly enjoy "Comus; " that all music
is lost to you, unless you delight in "Parsifal."
It is the special privilege of ethical criticism
to take this exclusive and didactic form; to
bid you admire a thing, not because it is beautiful in itself, but because it has a subtle lesson
to convey, — a lesson of which, it is urbanely
hinted, you stand particularly in need. On
precisely the same principle, you are com-
manded to cleave to Tolstoï, not because he
has written able novels, but because those
novels teach a great many things which it is
desirable you should know and believe; you
are bidden to revere George Meredith, not
because he has given the world some brilliant
and captivating books, but because these books
contain a tonic element fitted for your moral
reconstruction. If you do not sufficiently value
these admirable lessons, then you are told, in

language every whit as contemptuous as Mr.
Ruskin's, to amuse yourself, by all means, with
Lever, and Gaboriau, and Jules Verne; for
all, higher fiction is, like the art of Florence,
a sealed book to your understanding.

" Most men," says Mr. Froude, " feel the
necessity of being on some terms with their conscience, at their own expense or at another's ; "
and one very popular method of balancing their
score is by exacting from art and literature
that serious ethical purpose which they hesitate
to intrude too prominently into their daily lives,
rightly opining that it gives much less trouble
in books. So prevalent is this tone in modern thought that even a consummate critic like
Mr. Bagehot is capable of saying, in one of his
supremely moral moments, that Byron's poems
" taught nothing, and therefore are forgotten."
Et tu, Brute ! Such a sentence from such a
pen makes me realize something of the bitterness with which the dying Cæsar covered up his
face from his most trusted friend. That Lord
Byron's poems are forgotten is rather a matter
of doubt ; that they are given over entirely into
the hands of " a stray schoolboy " is a hazard-
ous assertion to make ; but to say that they are

forgotten *because* they teach nothing is to strike at the very life and soul of poetry. It does not exist to teach, but to please ; it can cease to exist only when it ceases to give pleasure.

Perhaps what Mr. Bagehot meant to imply is that it would be a difficult task to review Byron's poetry after the approved modern fashion ; to assign him, as we assign more contemplative and analytic poets, a moral *raison d'être.* Pick up a criticism of Mr. Browning, for example, and this is the first thing we see : " What was the kernel of Browning's ethical teaching, and how does he apply its principles to life, religion, art, and love ? " [1]  It would be as manifestly absurd to ask this question about Byron as it would be to review Fielding from the standpoint adapted for Tolstoï, or to discuss Sheridan from the same field of view as Ibsen. With the earlier writers it was a question of workmanship ; with our present favorites it has become a question of ethics. Yet when we seek for simple edification, as our plain-spoken grandfathers understood the word, as many innocent people understand it now, the new school seems as remote from fur-

[1] *Quarterly Review.*

nishing it as the old. Browning, Tolstoï, and Ibsen have their own methods of dealing with sin, and richly suggestive and illustrative methods they are. The lessons taught may be of a highly desirable kind, but I doubt their practical efficacy in our common working lives; and I cannot think this possible efficacy warrants their intrusion into art. Great truths, unconsciously revealed and as unconsciously absorbed, have been, in all ages, the soul of poetry, the subtle life of fiction. These truths, always in harmony with the natural world and with the vital sympathies of man, were not put forward crudely as lessons to be learned, but primarily as pleasures to be enjoyed; and through our " sweet content," as Burton phrased it, we came into our heritage of knowledge. To-day both poetry and fiction have assumed a different and less winning attitude. They have grown sensibly didactic, are at times almost reproachful in their tone, and, so far from striving to yield us pleasure, to increase our " sweet content " with life, they endeavor, with very tolerable success, to prevent our being happy after our own limited fashion. Their principal mission is to worry us vaguely

about our souls or our neighbors' souls, or the
social order which we did not establish, and the
painful problems that we cannot solve. Our
spirits, at all times restless and troubled, respond with quick alarm to these dismal agita-
tions; our serenity is not proof against the
strain; our sense of humor is not keen enough
to cure us with wholesome laughter; and nineteenth - century cultivation consists in being
miserable for misery's sake, and in saying
solemnly to one another at proper intervals,
" This is the eternal progress of the ages. "

It was a curious and rather melancholy experience, a year ago, to hear the comments of
those patient women who devoted their afternoons to Ibsen readings, and to turning over
in their minds the new and unprofitable situations thus suggested. The discussions that
followed were invariably ethical, never critical;
they had reference always to some moral co-
nundrum offered by the play, never to the artistic or dramatic excellence of the play itself.
Was Nora Helmer justified, or was she not, in
abandoning her children with explicit confidence to the care of Mary Ann? Had Dr.
Wangel a right, or had he not, to annul his

own marriage tie with the primitive simplicity
of the king of Dahomey? To answer such
questions as these has become our notion of
literary recreation, and there is something pa-
thetically droll in the earnestness with which
we bend our wits to the task. Indeed, poor
little Nora's matrimonial infelicities threatened to become as important in their way as
those of Catherine of Aragon or Josephine
Beauharnais, and we talked about them quite
seriously and with a certain awe. The un-
flinching manner in which Ibsen has followed
Sir Thomas Browne's advice, "Strive not to
beautify thy corruption!" commends him, naturally, to that large class of persons who can
tolerate sin only when it is dismal; and Bau-
delaire, praying for a new vice, was jocund
in comparison with our Norwegian dramatist,
unwearyingly analyzing the old one. Yet
what have we gained from the rankness of
these disclosures, from these horrible studies
of heredity, these hospital and madhouse
sketches, these incursions of pathology into the
realms of art? What shall we ever gain by
beating down the barriers of reserve which
civilized communities have thought fit to rear,

by abandoning that wholesome reticence which is the test of self-restraint? We try so hard to be happy, — we have such need, each of his little share of happiness ; yet Ibsen, troubling the soul more even than he troubles the senses, has chosen to employ his God-given genius in deliberately lessening our small sum of human joy. When shall we cease to worship at such dark altars? When shall we recognize, with Goethe, that "all talent is wasted if the subject be unsuitable"? When shall we understand and believe that "the gladness of a spirit is an index of its power"?

"To live," says Amiel, "we must conquer incessantly, we must have the courage to be happy." Enjoyment, then, is not our common daily portion, to be stupidly ignored or carelessly cast away. It is something we must seek courageously and intelligently, distinguishing the pure sources from which it flows, and rightly persuaded that art is true and good only when it adds to our delight. For this were our poets and dramatists, our painters and novelists, sent to us, — to make us lawfully happier in a hard world, to help us smilingly through the gloom. And can it be they think

this mission beneath their august consideration,
unworthy of their mighty powers? Why, to
have given pleasure to one human being is a
recollection that sweetens life; and what should
be the fervor and transport of him to whom it
has been granted to give pleasure to generations, to add materially to the stored-up gladness of the earth! "Science pales," says Mr.
Dallas, "age after age is forgotten, and age
after age has to be freshened; but the secret
thinking of humanity, embalmed in art, survives, as nothing else in life survives." This
is our inheritance from the past, — this secret
thinking of humanity, embalmed in imperishable beauty, and enduring for our delight.
The thinking of that idle vicar, Robert Herrick, when he sang, on a fair May morning: —

> " Come, let us go, while we are in our prime,
> And take the harmless folly of the time!
> We shall grow old apace, and die
> Before we know our liberty."

The thinking of Theocritus, who, lying drow-
sily on the hillside, saw the sacred waters well-
ing from the cool caverns, and heard the little
owl cry in the thorn brake, and the yellow bees
murmur and hum in the soft spicy air: —

" All breathed the scent of the opulent summer, of the season of fruit. Pears and apples were rolling at our feet; the tender branches, laden with wild plums, were bowed to earth; and the four-year-old pitch seal was loosened from the mouth of the wine-jars."

Here is art attuned to the simplest forms of pleasure, yet as lasting as the pyramids, — a whispered charm borne down the current of years to soothe our fretted souls. But the tranquil enjoyment of what is given us to enjoy has become a subtle reproach in these days of restless disquiet, of morbid and conscious self-scrutiny, when we have forfeited our sympathy with the beliefs, the aspirations, and the "sweet content" that linked the centuries together. We are suffering at present from a glut of precepts, a surfeit of preceptors, and have grown sadly wise, and very much cast down in consequence. We lack, as Amiel says, the courage to be happy, and glorify our discontent into an intellectual barrier, pluming ourselves on a seriousness that may not be diverted. But if we will only consent to calm our fears, to quiet our scruples, to humble our pride, and to take one glad look into the world

of art, we shall see it bathed in the golden sunlight of pleasure; and wè shall know very well
that didacticism, whether masquerading as a
psychological drama or a socialistic forecast,
as a Sunday-school story or a deistical novel,
is no guide to that enchanted land.

IT is one of the most delightful things about Miss Edgeworth's immortal tales for children that the incidents they relate have a knack of remaining indelibly fixed in our memories, long after we have succeeded in forgetting the more severely acquired information of our school-days. Why, for instance, do I vex my temper and break my finger-nails in a vain effort to untie the knotted cord of every bundle that comes to the house, save that I have still before me the salutary example of that prudent little Ben, who so conscientiously and cheerfully devoted himself to unfastening his uncle's package? "You may keep the string for your pains," says Mr. Gresham, with pleasing liberality. "Thank you, sir," replies Ben, with more effusion than I think he feels. "What an excellent whipcord it is!" And so, pocketing his fee, it wins for him, as we all know, the prize at Lady Diana Sweepstake's great archery contest, while poor Hal forfeits his shot,

and loses his hat, and gets covered with mud
and disgrace, and sprains his little cousin Pat-
ty's ankle, and all because he has been rash
enough to cut his piece of cord. Never was
moral more sternly pointed, not even in the
case of Miss Jane Taylor's heedless little
Emily, who will not stoop to pick up a pin, and
is punished by the loss of a whole day's pleasure, because, owing to some unexplained in-
tricacy of her toilet, —

> " She could not stir,
> For just a pin to finish her. "

But was whipcord such a costly article in
Miss Edgeworth's time, that a small piece of it
was worth so much trouble and pains? We
have Hal's testimony that twice as much could
have been bought for twopence; and though
Hal is but a graceless young scamp, who cannot be induced to look upon twopence with becoming reverence, and who plainly has a career
of want and misery before him, yet his word
on this matter may be accepted as final. At
the present day, the value of a bit of string
saved by patient dexterity from the scissors is
so infinitesimal that the hoarding up of match
stumps, after the fashion of a certain great

banker, would really seem the quicker road to wealth. But the true gain in these minute economies is of a strictly moral nature, and serves, when we know we have been extravagant, to balance our account with conscience. The least practical of us have some petty thrift dear to our hearts, some one direction in which we love to scrimp. I have known wealthy men who grudged themselves and their families nothing that money could buy, yet were made perfectly miserable by the amount of gas burned nightly in their homes. They roamed around with manifest and pitiful uneasiness, stealthily turning down a burner here and there, whenever they could do so unperceived, dimming the glories of their glass and gilding, and reducing upper halls and familiar stairways into very pitfalls for the stumbling of the unwary. The advent of lamps has brought but scant solace to these sufferers, for their economy is, in fact, much older than the gas itself, and flourished exceedingly in the days of wax tapers and tallow-dips. We read in the veracious chronicles of "Cranford" how Miss Matty Jenkyns, so thoughtlessly generous in all other matters, had for her one pet frugality the hoard-

ing of her candles, and by how many intricate
devices the dear old lady sought to cherish and
protect these objects of her tender solicitude.

"They (the candles) were usually brought
in with tea, but we only burned one at a time.
As we lived in constant preparation for a
friend who might come in any moment (but
who never did), it required some contriv-
ance to keep them of the same length, ready
to be lighted, and to look as if we burned two
always. They took it in turns, and, whatever
we might be talking about or doing, Miss
Matty's eyes were habitually fixed upon the
candle, ready to jump up and extinguish it,
and to light the other, before they had become
too uneven in length to be restored to equality
in the course of the evening."

This little scene of innocent deception is
finer, in its way, than the famous newspaper
paths on which Miss Deborah's guests step
lightly over her new carpet to their respective
chairs. We sympathize with Miss Matty's
anxiety about her tapers because it represents
one phase of a weakness common to all mankind, and far remote, we trust, from mere
vulgar parsimony, which, seeking to stint in all

things, is, by its very nature, incapable of a
nice spirit of selection. Even the narrator of
"Cranford," that shadowy, indistinguishable
Mary Smith, who contrives so cleverly to keep
her own identity in the background, — even she
consents to emerge one moment from her chosen
dimness, and to claim a share in this highly
discriminating economy. String, she acknowledges, is her foible. Like the excellent Mr.
Gresham, she would preserve it from destruction at the most liberal expenditure of other
people's time and trouble. "My pockets," she
confesses, "get full of little hanks of it, picked
up and twisted together, ready for uses that
never come. I am seriously annoyed if any
one cuts the string of a parcel instead of patiently and faithfully undoing it fold by fold.
How people can bring themselves to use India-
rubber rings, which are a sort of deification
of string, as lightly as they do, I cannot imagine. To me an India-rubber ring is a precious treasure. I have one which is not new ;
one that I picked up off the floor six years
ago. I have really tried to use it, but my
heart failed me, and I could not commit the
extravagance."

It would be a pity to spoil this vivacious description by a touch of odious modern realism, and to hint that an India-rubber ring which had knocked about the world for six years must have parted with much of its youthful elasticity, and would be of comparatively little use to any one.

Illustrious examples are not lacking to give dignity and weight to these seemingly trivial frugalities. The great, and wise, and mean Duke of Marlborough, he who held the fate of Europe in his hands, and who was, without doubt, the first of English-speaking generals, did not disdain to bend his mighty mind to the contemplation of his candle-ends, or to the tender protection of his luggage. Who understood so well as he how to spend a thousand pounds, and save a shilling? When Prince Eugene came to a conference in his tent, the duke's servant, anxious no doubt for an ostentatious display, had the temerity to light four wax tapers in honor of the royal guest, which, when Marlborough perceived, he promptly extinguished, rating the unlucky attendant with such caustic severity that the offense ran little likelihood of being soon repeated. While the great pile of Blenheim was absorbing countless thousands in its slow process of erection, the duke walked every morning from the public rooms at Bath to his own lodging, thereby saving sixpence daily, and affording a shining model to those whose favorite economy is cab-hire. He walked to the very end, this consistent old warrior; walked while the pangs of illness were creeping over his disabled frame; and at last, when he could save no more sixpences, he died, and left nearly two million pounds to be squandered briskly by his heirs.

His wife, too, the beautiful, brilliant, high-tempered Duchess Sarah, was every bit as thrifty as her lord. She built the triumphal arch of Blenheim at her own expense, and wrangled mightily all the while over the price of lime, "sevenpence half-penny per bushel, when it could be made in the park." She was the richest peeress in England, but her keen blue eyes, as fiery as Marlborough's own, were ever awake to any attempted depredation. Her dressmaker, one Mrs. Buda, essayed, not knowing with whom she had to deal, to hold back from her some yards of cloth; whereupon the duchess borrowed Mrs. Buda's diamond

ring "for a pattern," and refused to give it
up until the stuff was returned. She understood also the admirable art of utilizing her
friends, and there is a delighful letter written
by her to Lord Stair, then minister at France,
commissioning him to buy her a night-gown,
or more properly a dressing-gown, "easy and
warm, with a light silk wadd in it, such as are
used to come out of bed and gird round, without any train at all, but very full. 'T is no
matter what color, except pink or yellow — no
gold or silver in it; but some pretty striped
satin or damask, lined with a tafetty of the
same color." She also desires for her daughter, Lady Harriet, then a child of thirteen, "a
monto and petticoat to go abroad in, no silver
or gold in it, nor a stuff that is dear, but a
middling one that may be worn either in winter or in summer." The canny duchess pru-
dently adds that she will wait for the things
until "no one need be troubled with the custom-house people," a euphuism worthy of an
American conscience, and she thanks Lord
Stair at the same time for sending her "a pair
of bodyes," which were so well-fitting, and evidently so cheap, that she will have two more

pairs of "white tabby from the same taylor."
Fancy asking a foreign minister to purchase
one's stays, and wrappers, and little daughter's
petticoats, and to please wait his opportunity
to smuggle them in without duty!

Yet "Queen Sarah" was capable of sudden
deeds of generosity that quite take away our
breath by their magnificence, and so, for the
matter of that, was another noble termagant,
Queen Elizabeth, who gave away right royally
with one hand, even while she held out the
other for beggarly gratuities.   We see her
heaping riches into Sir Walter Raleigh's lap,
and managing to get a great deal of it back
again, when his treasure-laden ships came
slowly to port. ·  Nay, did she not seize on "a
waistcoat of carnation colour, curiously embroidered," which the brave navigator, always
passionately addicted to fine clothes, had
snatched from some Spanish galleon for the
adornment of his own handsome figure, and
which the queen straightway proceeded to
flaunt as a stomacher before his injured eyes?
If we read a list of Elizabeth's New Year gifts,
we are both astonished and edified by their
number and variety.  Here is Fulke Greville

presenting his sovereign with a night-dress; not
a wrapper this time, but a genuine night-dress,
" made of cambric, wrought about the collar
and sleeves with Spanish work of roses and
*letters*, and a night-coif with a forehead-cloth
of the same work." And here is Mrs. Carre
offering her majesty an embroidered cambric
sheet; and Dr. Bayly, one of the court physi-
cians, arriving brisk and early with a pot of
green ginger under his arm; and Mrs. Amy
Shelton with six handkerchiefs all edged with
gold and silver braid; and Sir Philip Sidney
with a most beautiful cambric smock, " and a
suite of ruffs of cut-work, flourished with gold
and silver, and set with spangles containing
four ounces of gold." And here, best of all,
are several gentlemen of rank, who, being unacquainted with the intricacies of the female
toilet, feel afraid to venture upon smocks, and
ruffs, and night-dresses, so solve their dilemma
by plumply handing down ten pounds apiece,
a practical donation which the virgin monarch
accepts with all possible alacrity and good-will.

Elizabeth, moreover, was known to be a
costly and often a sadly unremunerative guest
when it pleased her to visit her loyal people.

There is a letter written by the Earl of Bedford to Lord Burleigh that is positively pathetic in its apprehension of the impending honor. " I trust truly," says the expectant host, "that your lordship will have in remembrance to provide and help that her majesty's tarrying be not above two nights and a day, for so long time do I prepare." As it was one of the queen's whims to give scant warning of her coming, the unfortunate gentlemen suddenly called upon to harbor their sovereign and her suite often found themselves at their wits' end for food and entertainment; and not unfrequently it happened that, after days of ruinous expenditure, they had the satisfaction of seeing their prospects as blighted as their larders. Lord Henry Berkely lamenting the loss of his good red deer, twenty-seven of which were slain in one day — in their owner's absence, be it noted — for Elizabeth's diversion, was at least a happier man than the luckless young Rookwood of Euston Hall, whom her majesty requited for his hospitality by cruel insult and imprisonment. Even King John, who has come down to us in history as the least profitable of royal guests, could not well do worse than this,

though his visits, being occasionally of longer
duration, were just so much harder to be borne.
In the chronicles of Jocelin of Brakelond, we
read how once the king came with a large reti-
nue to the convent of St. Edmundsbury, and
stayed there for two whole weeks, eating up
the monks' provisions at a fearful rate, empty-
ing the cellars of their choicest wines, and
making, no doubt, what with drunken, swear-
ing soldiers and insolent court parasites, sad
riot and confusion within those peaceful walls.
At last, however, the weary fortnight was over,
and the guests stood marshaled to depart; but
not before his gracious majesty had made
offering, as guerdon for two weeks' entertainment, of a silk cloak to cover St. Edmund's
shrine, which same cloak was promptly borrowed back again by one of the royal train,
and the monks beheld it no more. In addition
to this elusive legacy, which left the shrine as
bare as it found it, Jocelin records that the
monarch, ere he rode forth, presented the convent with the handsome sum of thirteen pence,
in consideration of a mass being said for his
soul, which sorely needed all the spiritual ali-
ment the good monks could furnish it. We

can fancy Abbot Samson standing at his mon-
astery door, and regarding those thirteen pence
very much as the Genoese consul must have regarded the Duke of Kingston's old spectacles,
which the dowager duchess tendered him in
return for his hospitality ; or as Commodore
Barnet regarded the paste emerald ring with
which Lady Mary Wortley Montagu gracefully acknowledged the valuable services of
his man-of-war.

·  "Lady Mary's avarice seems to have been
generally credited at the time, though we have
no proofs of it," says one of her recent biogra-
phers, who is disposed, and rightly, to put
scant faith in Walpole's malicious jibes.  But
if the story of the ring be a true one, she can
hardly be acquitted of amazing thrift, and of
a still more amazing assurance.  It is said that
the gallant commodore, never doubting the
worth of her token, was wont to show it with
some ostentation to his friends, until one of
them, who knew the lady well, stoutly maintained that if the stone were genuine she would
never have parted with it, and a closer inspection proved the melancholy accuracy of his
suspicions.  As for much of her so-called

greed, it was not without solid justification.
If she drove a hard bargain with Mr. Wortley,
stipulating most unromantically for her marriage settlement before she ran away with him,
be it remembered that upon this auspicious
occasion she was compelled to act as her own
guardian; and if she had an inexplicable fancy
for wearing her old clothes, the dimity petticoat, and the gray stockings, and the faded
green brocade riding-jacket which so deeply
offended Walpole's fastidious eyes, let us deal
charitably with a fault in which she has but
few feminine successors. Those were times
when fashions had not yet learned to change
with such chameleon-like speed, and people did
occasionally wear their old clothes with an unblushing effrontery that would be well-nigh
disgraceful to-day. Silks and satins, laces and
furbelows, were all of the costliest description,
and their owners were chary of discarding
them, or even of lightly exposing them to ruin.
Emile Souvestre's languid lady, who proves
the purity of her blood, somewhat after the
manner of the princess and the rose leaf, by
supercilious indifference to the fate of her vel-
vet mantle in a snowstorm, could hardly have

existed a few hundred years ago.  We have in
Pepys's diary a most amusing record of his disgust at being over-persuaded by his wife to
wear his best suit on a certain threatening May
Day, and how of course it rained, and all their
pleasure was spoiled.  The guilty Eve was
quite as unfortunate as her husband, for she
too had gone forth "extraordinary fine in her
flowered tabby gown," which we are greatly
relieved to learn a little later was two years
old, but smartly renovated with brand-new
lacings.  Only fancy being so careful of a
two-year gown as to begrudge it to the sight
of court and commoners on May Day !

The same frugal spirit extended down to the
last century, and was of infinite value to the
self-respecting poor.  Artisans had not yet
found it imperative to dress their wives and
children in imitation finery, and farmers were
even less awake to the exigencies of fashionable attire.  We read of rural couples placidly
wearing their wedding clothes into their advanced old age, and we are lost in hopeless
speculation as to how they accommodated their
spreading proportions to the coats and gowns
which presumably had fitted the comparative

slimness of their youth. With what patient
ingenuity did the good dames of Miss Mitford's
village, aided occasionally by an itinerant tai-
loress, turn and return their husbands' cast-off
clothing, until, from seeming ruin, they had
evolved sound garments for their growing boys;
and with what pardonable pride did the strut-
ting youngsters exhibit on the village streets
these baggy specimens of their mothers' skill!
Among the innumerable anecdotes told of
George III., it is said that, strolling once with
Queen Charlotte in the woods of Windsor, he
met a little red-cheeked, white-haired lad, who
proved, on examination, to be the son of one of
his majesty's beef-eaters. The gracious king,
always well pleased with children, patted the
boy's flaxen head, and bade him kneel and kiss
the queen's hand, but this the sturdy young
Briton declined flatly to do ; not, be it said, from
any desire to emulate the examples of Penn and
Franklin, by illustrating on a minor scale the
heroic principles of democracy, but solely and
entirely that he might not spoil his new
breeches by contact with the grass. So thrifty
a monarch, says Thackeray, should have hugged
on the spot a child after his own heart; and

even if the royal favor failed to manifest itself in precisely this fashion, I make no doubt that the beef-eater's wife, who had stitched those little breeches with motherly solicitude, found ample comfort in such a judicious son.

Perhaps, indeed, he was a worthy scion of the race of Dodsons, with whom it was an honorable tradition to preserve their best clothes, very much as the inhabitants of Ceylon preserved their sacred Bo-trees, by guarding them jealously from the desecrating touch of man. Who that has ever had the happiness of reading " The Mill on the Floss " can forget the dim seclusion of the shrouded room, where, far from the madding crowd, reposes in dignified seclusion Mrs. Pullet's new bonnet? To go to see it is in itself a pilgrimage ; to try it on, a solemn ceremonial ; what, then, must have been the profound emotions with which it was actually worn ! Little Maggie Tulliver, watching with breathless interest while it is lifted reverently from the shrine, feels oppressed with a sense of mystery, and is childishly indignant because no one will tell her what it means. The Dodsons are all fond of fine raiment, but not for the mere vulgar pleasure of

self-adornment. Less favored families may take
a coarse delight in exhibiting their clothes, but
it remains for them to derive a higher gratification from keeping them unseen. Even a
third-best front is felt to be much too good for
a sister's dinner party, while in the matter of
frocks and trimmings they are as adamant.
" Other women, if they liked, might have their
best thread lace in every wash ; but when Mrs.
Glegg died, it would be found that she had
better lace laid by in the right-hand drawer of
her wardrobe in the spotted chamber, than ever
Mrs. Wooll of St. Ogg's had bought in her life,
although Mrs. Wooll wore her lace before it was
paid for." Here, in a humble way, we have
the same sentiment that thrilled the heart of
Elizabeth Petrovna, when she gazed at the
thousand and one gowns hanging up in the
royal closets, and felt a true womanly satisfaction in knowing they were there.

It is in fact a curious and edifying circumstance that the great ones of this earth, if they
must be held responsible for much of its unwarranted luxury, have at the same time afforded us many shining examples, not only of
that general and indiscriminate parsimony

which induced old Frederic William, for instance, to feed his family on pork and cabbage,
but also of that more refined and esoteric
species of economy which it is our task to recognize and encourage.   George III. was frugal
in all things, but his particular saving appears
to have been in carpets, for, summer or winter,
he never permitted these effeminate devices
upon his bedroom floor.   His great - grand-
father, George I., does not figure as an austere
or self-denying character; but he, too, stinted
bravely in one direction, — the family wash.
In that beloved court of Hanover, which he
exchanged so reluctantly for the glories of St.
James, there was evidently no lack of well-fed,
well-paid attendants.   Looking down the list,.
we see seventy odd postilions and stable-men,
twenty cooks with six assistants, seven " officers
of the cellar," twenty-four lackeys in livery,
sixteen trumpeters and fiddlers, — and only
two washerwomen.   Think of it, — twenty-six
people to cook, and only two to wash !   " But
one half-pennyworth of bread to this intoler-
able deal of sack ! "   Yet the chances are that,
of all the officials in that snug, jolly, dirty little
Hanoverian   court, those   two   washerwomen

alone led comparatively idle lives. When
balanced with the arduous labors of the seven
officers of the cellar, I am convinced their
position was a sinecure.

Of much the same temper as royal George
was that great Earl of Northumberland,
whose expense-book, which may be consulted
to-day, gives us a delightful insight into some
of the curious methods of past housekeeping.
Germany, be it confessed, has always been
a trifle backward in the matter of cleanli-
ness, but England, until within the last two
centuries, was very nearly as conservative.
Appalling stories are told of the fine ladies
and gentlemen who glittered in the courts of
the Tudors and Stuarts, and who, in their
light-hearted indifference to dirt, very nearly
rivaled the prowess of the Spanish Isabella,
when she vowed away her clean linen until
Ostend should fall, and gave the honor of her
name to that delicate yellow tint which her
garments assumed in the interval. The Earl
of Northumberland, however, aspired to no
such uneasy asceticism. He was simply the
model housekeeper of his age. Every item of
expenditure in his immense establishment was

rigorously defined, and no less rigorously over-
looked. With his own noble hands he wrote
down the exact proportion of food, fuel, and
candles which each body of retainers was expected to consume ; and while the upper servants appear to have fared tolerably well, the
commoner sort enjoyed an unbroken monotony
of salt meat, black bread, and beer. But it
is in the matter of tablecloths that his grace
chiefly excelled, and that he merits an honorable mention in the ranks of esoteric parsimony.
For his own needs, and for the service and
pleasure of his many guests, — and let us remember that he kept open house after the hos-
pitable fashion of his day, — eight of these
valuable articles were deemed amply sufficient ;
while in the servants' hall one cloth a month was
the allowance. Granted, if you please, that in
this rather effeminate age we have grown unduly fastidious about such trivialities ; yet who,
looking back through the long vista of years,
can contemplate without a shudder the condition of that tablecloth when its month's servitude was over ?

It is easier, however, to jeer at the honorable
efforts of mankind than to arrange our own

economies on a strictly satisfactory basis.· Beyond a rational and healthy impulse to save on others rather than on ourselves, few of us can boast of much enlightenment in the matter, and even our one unerring guide is, in a measure, neutralized by the consistent determination of others to exert their own saving powers on us. The out-and-out miser is at best a creature of little penetration. He cheats himself sorely throughout life, and gains a sort of shabby posthumous distinction only when he is long past enjoying it. The true economist is, if we may believe Mrs. Oliphant, a *rara avis*, as exceptional in his way as the true genius. She endeavors, indeed, with much humility, to describe for us such a character in " The Curate in Charge ; " but, while laying all possible stress on Mrs. St. John's extraordinary proficiency, she does not for a moment venture to hint at the secret of her power. " I don't pretend to know how she did it," confesses this discriminating authoress, " any more than I can tell you how Shakespeare wrote ' Hamlet.' It was quite easy to him and to her, but if one knew how, one would be as great a poet as he was, as great an economist as she."

This is a degree of perfection to which we may not well aspire.    Shakespeare and Mrs. St. John lie equally beyond our humble imitation. We do not even feel ambitious of such excellence, but cherish the more contentedly those few finely selected frugalities, those car-fares and match-stumps, those postage stamps and half sheets of paper, those dimly-lighted rooms and evaded custom-house duties, which, while they may not leave us much richer at the year's end, have yet a distinct ethical value of their own, and, breathing an indescribable air of conscious rectitude, serve to keep us in harmony with ourselves.

## SCANDERBEG.

CLIO is the most shamelessly unreliable of the Muses. She selects her favorites with the autocratic partiality of the Russian Catherine, decorates them with questionable honors, enriches them with other people's spoils, admires them to her heart's content, and thrusts them serenely to the front to receive the approbation of the world. Occasionally she wearies of one or the other, and flings him lightly down from the pedestal he has adorned so bravely. Occasionally, having a fine feminine sense of humor, she is pleased to play with our credulity, and, dressing up a man of straw, she assures us smilingly that he is real flesh and blood, and worthy of our sincerest admiration. And all this while, her best and noblest meet with stiffly measured praise, and her strong sons are passed indifferently by. It is at least amusing to think of the relative positions occupied by the true mountaineer Scanderbeg, and the mythical mountaineer William Tell. The

one sleeps unremembered with scanty, hard-
won fame ; the other carries such a weight of
laurels that poets, wearied with singing his
praises, have been driven in despair to sing the
praises of those who praise him, as Coleridge
piped to the Duchess of Devonshire, —

"Splendor's fondly fostered child,"

because, in a moment of mild enthusiasm, she
addressed some well-meant but highly inefficient
verses to the platform from which Tell did not
shoot the tyrant Gessler.

If the heroic struggle for a national life is
at all times the most engrossing picture the
world's history has to show us, where shall we
look for a more vivid illustration of the theme
than in the long and bitter contest between
cross and crescent, between the steady, relentless encroachment of the Turkoman power, and
the vain and dauntless courage which opposed
it? The story of the early Ottomans is one of
wasteful and inexorable conquest, unrelieved
by any touches of humanity, or any impulses
towards a higher civilization. To the ferocious
and impetuous pride of the barbarian they
added an almost inconceivable wariness and

patience; they knew when to wait and when
to strike; they were never unduly elated by
victory, and never demoralized by defeat.
That strange dream of their founder Othman
which won for him his Cilician wife, the mysterious vision of the full moon resting in his
bosom, and of the stately tree that sprang
therefrom, must have dimly hinted to the savage chief of the glory that was to be. When
in his sleep he placed Constantinople as a
jewel upon his swarthy finger, he felt the
coming of shrouded things, and, believing the
prophecy would be fulfilled in his descendant,
he saluted his bride as the mother of a mighty
race of kings. It was this firm conviction of
future greatness which made him seek for his
son Orchan a fairer and nobler wife than
could be found in the black tents of his followers; and, true to the instincts of his race,
he despoiled an enemy to enrich his own hearth.
A Greek captain, in command of the castle of
Belecoma, was betrothed to the beautiful
daughter of a neighboring Christian chief.
On their marriage night Othman surprised
the wedding party as they rode through the
dark mountain passes. The short and desper-

ate conflict which ensued could have but one
bitter ending.  " The bridegroom was slain,
and his Greek bride, the Lotus-flower of Brusa,
was swept off by the Turkoman robbers to
their lair, to become the spouse of their leader's
son. " [1]

Orchan was a mere boy when he received this
ravished prize, the fair booty of a barbarous
strife.  Fifty years later, when hair and beard
were white with age, he married again; and
this time his bride was the daughter of a Christian emperor, not stolen away from friends and
kindred, but given to him publicly with superb
ceremonies, and a ghastly mockery of rejoicing.
In fifty years the Ottoman power had grown
into such fierce and sinister lustihood that
Theodora, daughter of the Emperor Cantacu-
zene, was assigned as a precious hostage and
seal of friendship between her father and his
dreaded Turkish ally.  The church refused
her blessing to this unholy sacrifice, and, amid
the pomp and majesty of imperial nuptials,
there was lacking even the outward form of
Christian marriage.  From that date the tide
of Turkish conquest spread with devastating

[1] *The Early Ottomans*, by Dean Church.

rapidity. The impetuous encroachments of
Orchan, the steady and irresistible advances
of Amurath, became under Bajazet a struggle
for life and death, not with the enfeebled
powers of Greece, but with a rival conqueror
who had swept from the broad Tartar steppes
to subdue and lay waste the Eastern world.
Eight dynasties had already been destroyed,
eight crowned heads had been laid low, when
Timour, grimly ready for a ninth victim, encountered the hitherto invincible sultan. They
met, and Bajazet, who had seen the flower of
French and German chivalry perish at his command, who had sat at his tent-door to witness
the day-long massacre of Christian prisoners,
and who had shadowed the very walls of Constantinople, — Bajazet was crushed like a worm
by the lame, white-haired old Tartar, and, eating out his heart with dull fury, died in shameful captivity. But his race survived, vigorous,
elastic, defiant, and renewed its strength with
amazing swiftness under Mahommed the Re-
storer and Amurath the Second, whose reign
was one long conflict with the Greek Emperor
Manuel, with Sigismund of Hungary, and,
hardest of all to subdue, with those warlike

Sclavonic tribes who, often defeated but never conquered, maintained with superb courage the freedom of their mountain fastnesses. It was an unknown Servian soldier who slew Amurath the First in the very moment of his triumph; it was the Albanian chief Scanderbeg who repulsed Amurath the Second, and hurled him back to die, shamed and heart-broken, at Adrianople.

Pride of race, love for his native land, shame at prolonged captivity, and fury at heaped-up wrongs, — all these conflicting passions united themselves in the breast of this implacable warrior, and urged him relentlessly along his appointed path. He was the outcome of that ruthless policy by which the Turks turned the children of the cross into defenders of the crescent, a policy pursued with almost undeviating success since Black Halil, a century and a half before, had urged the training of Christian boys into a school of Moslem soldiers. What gives to the history of Scanderbeg its peculiar significance, and its peculiar ethical and artistic value is the fact that he avenged, not only his own injuries, but the injuries of countless children who, for over a hundred and fifty years, had been snatched from their homes, families, and faith to swell the ranks of an infidel foe. Wherever the tide of Ottoman battle raged most fiercely, there, savage, dark, invincible, stood the Janissaries, men suckled on Christian breasts and signed with Christian baptism, now flinging away their lives for an alien cause and an alien creed, fighting with the irresistible courage of fanaticism against their birthright and their kindred. Never before or since, in the history of all the nations, has a system of proselytizing been attended with such tremendous results. The life-blood of Christendom was drained to supply fresh triumphs for its enemies, and the rigorous discipline of a monastic training moulded these innocent young captives into a soldiery whose every thought and every action was subordinate to one overpowering influence, an austere, unquestioning obedience to the cause of Islam.

With the example of this extraordinary success always before their eyes, it is little wonder that the Turks regarded the children of the vanquished as so many docile instruments to be fashioned by rigid tutelage into faithful followers of the Prophet, and the first step

towards this desired goal lay in their early adop-
tion of the Mohammedan faith.  No pang of
pity, no sentiment of honor, interfered with this
relentless purpose.  When John Castriota, the
hereditary lord of Croia, yielded up his four
sons as hostages to Amurath the Second, he
relied on the abundant promises made him by
that sovereign, who had, on the whole, a fair
reputation for keeping his royal word.  The
lads were carried to Adrianople and reared in
the sultan's palace, where one at least of the
little prisoners attracted dangerous notice by
his vivacity and grace, — inheritances, it is
said, from his beautiful mother, Voisava.  The
fair-haired boy, then only eight years old, became first the plaything of the seraglio, and
afterwards the jealously guarded favorite of
Amurath himself.  He was carefully taught,
and was forced to conform to the ceremonial
rites of the Ottomans, and to make an open
profession of his new creed, receiving on this
occasion the name of Scanderbeg, a name destined to carry with it a just retribution in the
universal terror it excited.  How much of
Christian belief still lingered in the child's
soul, or how much he gained afterwards from

the Albanian soldiers who had access to him, it is impossible to say. Young as he was, he had learned, amid the unutterable treachery and corruption of an Eastern court, to hide his emotions under an impenetrable mask, so that even Amurath, cruel, wily, and suspicious, found himself baffled by this Greek boy, whose handsome face betrayed to none the impetuous anger that consumed him. At nineteen he had command of five thousand horsemen, and enjoyed the title of pasha, a barren honor for one soon to be robbed of his birthright. After the close of the Hungarian war John Castriota died, and Amurath, ignoring his plighted faith, seized Croia in the name of the captive princes, ruthlessly extinguished its civil and religious liberties, turned the churches into mosques, and treated the whole country as a defeated and dependent province. Scander-beg's three brothers were conveniently re-moved by poison; he himself, the object of a curious affection on the sultan's part, was watched with jealous and exacting eyes, and for a while it seemed as though the free-born mountain chief would add one more to the long list of Turkish proselytes and favorites, silenced with doubtful titles, bought with dishonorable wealth.

But it was a time of waiting, a time ominous with delay. The heir of Croia, mute, patient, and resolved, bided with steady self-control the hour when he could strike a single blow for faith and freedom. It came with the breaking out of fresh Hungarian troubles : with the defiance sent by John Hunyadi and his forces drawn up on the banks of the Moravia. While the Ottoman armies were engaged in this most disastrous conflict, Scanderbeg threw off his long-endured disguise, possessed himself by an unscrupulous device of his native city, and put all who opposed him to the sword. From that day until his death, forty years later, the record of his life is one perpetual heroic struggle to preserve the hard-won liberty of Epeiros, a struggle without intermission or relief, without rest for the victor or pity for the vanquished. His scornful indifference to pressing dangers was in itself the best of tonics to a people naturally brave, but taught by bitter experience to fear the inexorable Turkish yoke. Scanderbeg feared nothing ; with him, indeed, fear was swallowed up in hatred. He

understood perfectly the nature of the warfare
in which he was engaged; he knew that, with
adroitness and vigilance, every dark pass and
every rocky crag became his friend and ally.
He knew, too, the slender resources of the
country, and never committed the mistake of
taking more men into the field than he could
manage and support. When Amurath sent
an army of forty thousand soldiers to punish
Croia, and bring back the rebel chief "alive
or dead" to Adrianople, Scanderbeg limited
his own forces to seven thousand foot and eight
thousand horse, when he might, had he chosen,
have trebled that number. With this compact
body of picked and hardy warriors he lay in
wait for the enemy, entrapped them by a feigned
retreat into a narrow defile, and, hemming
them in on either side, filled up the valley with
their slain. Over twenty thousand Turks
perished in that dreadful snare, many of them
being trampled down by their helpless and
panic-stricken countrymen. It was Scanderbeg's first decisive victory, and a grim warning
to Amurath of the possibilities that awaited
him in the future. It gave to Croia a breathing spell, and to its victorious army the rich

spoils of an Ottoman camp, so that those who had gone forth meagrely on foot returned well armed and bravely mounted to their rock-built citadel.

Had this sudden and bewildering success been followed up by a vigorous aggressive warfare on the part of Servia, Hungary, and Poland, then all in arms against their common foe; had the allied powers listened to the mountain chiefs, or to the burning remonstrances of Cardinal Julian, the pope's legate, the Turks might have been driven forcibly back from Europe, and long centuries of suffering and dishonor spared to Christendom. But the lord of Servia, George Brankovich, yearned for his children whom Amurath held as hostages; Ladislaw, king of Hungary and Poland, was weary of the perpetual strife; even Hunyadi's fiery voice was silenced; and a treaty of peace was signed with an enemy who might then, and then only, have been crushed. This treaty, shameful in itself, was still more shamefully broken in the following year, when the Christian hosts again took the field, only to be utterly routed in the terrible battle of St. Martin's Eve. Never was disaster more com-

plete: Ladislaw's severed head, borne on a pike
over the Ottoman ranks, struck terror and despair into the hearts of his followers ; Hunyadi, after a vain, furious effort to redeem this
ghastly symbol of defeat, fled from a field red
with his countrymen's blood ; the papal legate
and two Hungarian bishops perished in the
thickest of the fray.   It was the beginning
of the end, and four years later the cause of
Christendom received its deathblow at Kos-
sova, when Hunyadi, beaten finally back from
Servia, was taught by the bitterness of defeat
that his name no longer sounded ominously,
as of old, in the ears of his Moslem foe.   Only
Scanderbeg remained unsubdued amid his
mountain peaks, and Amurath, flushed with
conquest, now turned his whole attention to
the final punishment of this audacious rebel.

The scale on which the invasion of Croia
was planned shows in itself how deep-seated
was the sultan's anger, and how relentless his
purpose.   One hundred and sixty thousand
men were assembled in Adrianople, the ablest
generals were united in command, and Mohammed, his savage son and successor, accom-
panied the expedition, filled with fierce hopes

of vengeance. Resistance seemed almost vain,
but Scanderbeg, in no way disturbed by the
coming storm, prepared with characteristic
coolness to meet it at every point. He ordered
all who dwelt in the open country or in unpro-
tected villages to destroy their harvests and to
quit their homes, so that the enemy might find
no resources in the scorched and deserted fields.
The women and children, the aged and infirm,
were sent either to the sea-coast or out of the
kingdom, many of them as far away as Venice.
The fortifications of Croia were repaired;
the garrison was strengthened and put under
command of a brave and able governor, and
Scanderbeg himself, with only ten thousand
men, took the field, ready to waylay and harass
Amurath at every step of his difficult and dangerous march. The first severe fighting was
done before the walls of Setigrade, a strongly
guarded town which made a gallant resistance,
repulsing the Turks again and again, and only
yielding when a traitor, bought by the sultan's
gold, poisoned the fountains which supplied
the city with water. From this point the in-
vading army marched on to Croia, covered the
surrounding plains, planted their cannon —

then an imposing novelty in warfare — before
its massive gates, and summoned the garrison
to surrender. A defiant refusal was returned ;
the Ottomans stormed the walls, and were repulsed with such fury that over eight thousand
Janissaries perished in the combat, while
Scanderbeg, poised like an eagle on the cliffs,
waited until the battle was at its height, and
then sweeping down on the unconscious foe,
forced their trenches, fired the camp, and drove
all before him with terrible havoc and slaugh-
ter. By the time Mohammed could rally his
scattered forces, the Epeirots were off and
away, with little scathe or damage to themselves ; and this exasperating method of attack
was the weapon with which the mountain chief
finally wore out the courage and endurance
of the invaders. Every inch of ground was
familiar to him, and a snare to his enemies.
Did Mohammed, burning with rage, scale the
hills in pursuit, a handful of men held him at
bay ; while Scanderbeg, appearing as if by
magic on the other side of the camp, chose this
propitious moment for an attack. By day or
night he gave the enemy no truce, no respite,
no quarter. Two hours out of the twenty-four

he slept, and all the rest he spent in unceasing, unwearying, unpitying warfare; until the Turks, harassed by a danger ever present but never visible, lost heart and trembled before the breathless energy of their foe. They were beginning also to suffer from a scarcity of provisions, and Scanderbeg took excellent care that this trouble should not be too speedily relieved. The supplies, brought at an immense cost from Desia, were intercepted and carried off triumphantly to the hills, and the unhappy Ottomans, starved in camp and slaughtered out of it, realized with ever-increasing dismay the unenviable nature of their position.

It must be admitted, in justice to the Epeirots, that the success of Scanderbeg's manœuvres rested exclusively on their absolute and unquestioned fidelity. Swift and sure information was brought him of every movement on the enemy's part, and vigilant eyes kept watch over every rocky pass that gave access to his haunts. For once Amurath's gold was powerless to buy a single traitor, and the systematic perfidy by which the Turks were accustomed to steal what they could not grasp failed for once of its prey. After a fruitless effort

to undermine the rock on which Croia was
founded, the sultan sought to corrupt first the
governor and then the garrison with dazzling
offers of advancement, but all the wealth in
Adrianople could not purchase one poor Christian soldier. Baffled and heart-sick with repeated failure, Amurath at last offered to raise
the siege and depart, on payment of a small
yearly sum, a mere nominal tribute to salve
his wounded pride. Even this trifling conces-
sion was sternly refused by Scanderbeg, who
would yield nothing to his hated foe. Then
for the first time the sultan understood the
relentless nature of this man whom he had
petted as a child and wronged as a boy, whom
he had held a helpless hostage in his hands,
and who now defied him with unutterable aversion and scorn. Abandoning himself to grief,
fury, and despair, he tore his white beard, and
recalled his countless triumphs in the past,
only to compare them with this shameful over-
throw. He who had seen the allied powers of
Christendom suing at his feet, to be humbled
in his old age by an insignificant Illyrian
chieftain! The blow broke his proud heart,
and on his death-bed he conjured his son to

avenge his name and honor. Gladly Mohammed undertook the task, but the present was
no time for its fulfillment. The siege of Croia
was raised, the dejected Moslem army strag-
gled homewards, cruelly harassed at every
step by their unwearied foe, and Scanderbeg
once more entered his native city amid the
acclamations of a brave people, born again
to freedom, and wild to welcome their de-
liverer.

It is pleasant to think that, before being
called a third time into the field, even this in-
domitable fighter found a little leisure in which
to marry a wife, and to cultivate the arts of
peace. Domestic tranquillity ran but a slender
chance of palling on its possessor in those stirring days; but Scanderbeg made the most of
his limited opportunities. He carried his
bride in triumph to every corner of his little
kingdom, he labored hard to restore those
habits of thrift and industry which perpetual
warfare roots out of every nation, and he
wisely refrained from overtaxing the narrow
resources of his people. When his purse was
empty, he looked to his enemies and not to his
friends for its replenishment; and that stout

old adage, "The Turk's dominions are Scanderbeg's revenues," is a sufficient witness to
his admirable financiering. He realized fully
that the legacy of hate bequeathed by Amurath
to Mohammed would bear bitter fruits in the
hands of that fierce and able monarch, and so
employed every interval of peace in strength-
ening himself for the struggle that was to follow. Twice again during his lifetime was
Epeiros invaded by the Ottomans; and Scanderbeg, driven from his lair, was hunted like a
deer from hill to hill, now lying in covert, now
fiercely resisting, but unconquered always.
Wily offers of friendship from the sultan were
received with a not unnatural suspicion, and
courteously declined; hired assassins were de-
tected, and delivered up to a prompt and pitiless justice. For forty years this Albanian
soldier defended his mountain eyrie from a
power vast enough to destroy two empires,
and cruel enough to make the whole Eastern
world tremble. Constantinople fell, while
Croia stood unharmed. The last news brought
to Scanderbeg, as he lay dying at Lyssa, was
that the Turks had invaded the Venetian dominions. The feeble warrior raised himself in

bed, and called for his sword and armor. " Tell them," he gasped, " that I will be with them to-morrow," and fell back fainting on his pillows. On the morrow he was dead.

SANDWICHES, oranges, and penny novelettes
are the three great requisites for English traveling, — for third-class traveling, at least; and,
of the three, the novelette is by far the most
imperative, a pleasant proof of how our intellectual needs outstrip our bodily requirements.
The clerks and artisans, shopgirls, dressmakers, and milliners, who pour into London every
morning by the early trains, have, each and
every one, a choice specimen of penny fiction
with which to beguile the short journey, and
perhaps the few spare minutes of a busy day.
The workingman who slouches up and down
the platform, waiting for the moment of departure, is absorbed in some crumpled bit of
pink-covered romance. The girl who lounges
opposite to us in the carriage, and who would
be a very pretty girl in any other conceivable
hat, sucks mysterious sticky lozenges, and
reads a story called " Mariage à la Mode, or
Getting into Society," which she subsequently

lends to me, — seeing, I think, the covetous looks I cast in its direction, — and which I find gives as vivid and startling a picture of high life as one could reasonably expect for a penny. Should I fail to provide myself with one of these popular journals at the book-stall, another chance is generally afforded me before the train moves off ; and I am startled out of a sleepy reverie by a small boy's thrusting " A Black Business " alarmingly into my face, while a second diminutive lad on the platform holds out to me enticingly " Fettered for Life," " Neranya's Revenge," and " Ruby." The last has on the cover an alluring picture of a circus girl jumping through a hoop, which tempts me to the rashness of a purchase, circus riders being my literary weakness. I remember, myself, trying to write a story about one, when I was fourteen, and experiencing great difficulty from a comprehensive and all-embracing ignorance of my subject. It is but fair to the author of " Ruby " to say that he was too practiced a workman to be disconcerted or turned from his course by any such trivial disadvantage.

I should hardly like to confess how many

coins of the realm I dissipated before learning the melancholy truth, that the seductive
titles and cuts which form the *tours de force*
of penny fiction bear but a feeble affinity to
the tales themselves, which are like vials of
skimmed milk, labeled absinthe, but warranted
to be wholly without flavor. Mr. James Payn,
who has written very amusingly about the
mysterious weekly journals which lie "thick
as autumnal leaves that strew the brooks in Val-
lombrosa " upon the counters of small, dark
shops, "in the company of cheap tobacco,
hardbake, and, at the proper season, valen-
tines," laments with frank asperity that he can
find in them neither dramatic interest, nor even
impropriety. He has searched them patiently
for something wrong, and his quest has been
wholly unrewarded. Mr. Thomas Wright, in
a paper published some years ago in the " Nineteenth Century," makes a similar complaint.
The lovely heroines of these stories are " virtuous even to insipidity," and their heroes are so
blamably blameless as to be absolutely revolting. Yet it has been my fate to encounter
some very pretty villains in the course of my
penny readings, and at least one specimen of

the sinful gilded youth, who has "handsome blonde hair parted in the middle, a discontented mustache, a pale face and apathetic expression." This scion of the aristocracy, I am grieved to say, keeps beautiful Jewesses on board his sumptuous yacht, and otherwise misbehaves himself after a fashion calculated to make his relatives and well-wishers more discontented even than his mustache. He has a lovely sister, Alma, with whom, we are assured, the Prince of Wales danced three times in one night, "and was also heard to express his admiration of her looks and her *esprit* in some very emphatic superlatives, exciting a variety of comment and criticism." Naturally, and all the more naturally because the fair Alma discreetly reserves her *esprit* for royal ears and royal commendation, and is exceedingly chary of revealing any of it to interested readers, who are fain to know what kind of conversation the Prince found so diverting. From the specimens presented to our consideration, we are forced to conclude either that his Highness is easily satisfied in the matter of *esprit*, or that he has an almost superhuman power of detecting it when hidden from ordinary observation.

The wonderful dullness of penny fiction is not really due to the absence of incidents, of vice, or even of dramatic situations, but to the placidity with which these incidents or situations are presented and received. How can we reasonably be expected to excite ourselves over a catastrophe which makes little or no impression on the people most deeply concerned in it? When Bonny Adair engages herself, with guileless alacrity, to a man who has a wife already, the circumstance is narrated with a coolness which hardly allows of a tremor. The wife herself is not the hidden, mysterious, veiled creature with whom we are all familiar; not an actress, or a ballet girl, or an adventuress; but a highly respectable young lady, going into society, and drinking tea with poor Bonny at afternoon receptions. This would seem like a startling innovation, but as nobody else expresses any surprise at the matter, why should we? Bonny herself, it is explained, put no embarrassing questions to her suitor. "She was only a simple country maid. She knew that he loved her, and that was all she cared for." Still, to drink tea amicably with the wife of her *prétendu* is too much even for

a simple country maid ; and when Bonny is
formally introduced to " Mrs. Aleo Doyle," she
feels it time to withdraw from the scene and
become a hospital nurse, until a convenient
accident in the hunting-field removes the intrusive spouse, and reëstablishes her claim to
the husband.

The same well-bred indifference is revealed
in a more sensational story called " Elfrida's
Wooing," where we have a villainous uncle
foiled in his base plots ; a father supposed to
be drowned, but turning up just at the critical
moment ; a wicked lover baffled, a virtuous
lover rewarded. This sounds promising, but
in reality everything is taken with such wonderful calm that not a ripple of excitement
breaks over the smooth surface of the tale.
There is even an abduction, which surely cannot be an every-day occurrence in English
clerical life, — I do not remember anything
like it in one of Trollope's novels, — and by
mistake the wrong girl, the vicar's daughter, is
carried off by the rogues. But no matron of
feudal times could have betrayed less annoyance at the incident than does the vicar's wife.
" Rupert," she remarks placidly to her son, " it

is your place to go and look for your sister."
" Where shall I go ? " is the brother's languid
query. To which his mother retorts, with some
fretfulness : " How can I tell you ? If I knew,
I should be able to send for her myself," — a
very simple and a very sensible way of stating
the case ; but it sounds as if the pet dog, rather
than the only daughter of the family, had been
spirited suddenly away.

The most striking instance, however, of that
repose of mien which stamps the caste of
penny-fiction characters I found in a delightful
little romance entitled " Golden Chains," where
the heroine marries the villain to oblige a
friend, and is rewarded for her amiability by
being imprisoned in a ruined castle, situated
vaguely "on a lonely hillside looking down
upon the blue Mediterranean." Apparently,
nothing can be easier than to dispose of superfluous wives in this particular locality of Italy,
for no impertinent questions are asked ; and
Ernestine, proving intractable, is left by her
husband, Captain Beamish, an English officer
of a type not yet elucidated by Rudyard Kip-
ling, to starve quietly in her dungeon. She is
prevented from fulfilling this agreeable des-

tiny by the accidental drowning of the captain,
and the accidental arrival of her lover, — the
virtuous hero,—who is traveling providentially
in the south of Europe, and who has a taste for
exploring ruins.    This gentlemanly instinct
leads to the discovery of his beloved in a coma-
tose condition, " but beautiful still," though
" her youthful roundness was gone forever."
Surely now, the reader thinks, there will be a
scene of transport, of fierce wrath, of mingled
agony and rapture.    Nothing of the sort.
Linden merely " lifts the fair head upon his
arm," and administers a dose of brandy.    Then,
as Ernestine's eyes open, he murmurs, " ' Dearest, do you know me ? '    ' Yes,' she faintly
answered.    ' All is well, Nessa.    You have
been cruelly used, but all is well.    You are
safe with me.    Tell me, dear one, you are glad
to see me.' "

If she were not glad to see him, under the
circumstances, it would indicate an extraordinary indifference, not so much to love as to life ;
and the modesty which, in such a case, could
doubt a hearty welcome seems like an exagger-
ated emotion.    But the hero of penny fiction
is the least arrogant of mortals.    He worships

from afar, and expresses his affection in language which at times is almost obsequious in its timidity. He is never passionate, never exultant, never the least bit foolish, and never for a single moment relapses into humanity. Yet millions of people believe in him, love him, cherish him, and hail his weekly reappearance with sincere and unwearied applause.

The Unknown Public, that huge body of readers who meddle not with Ruskin, nor with Browning, nor with Herbert Spencer, who have no acquaintance with George Eliot, and to whom even Thackeray and Scott are as recondite as George Meredith and Walter Pater, has been an object of interest and curiosity to its neighbor, the Known Public, ever since Wilkie Collins formally introduced it into good society, more than thirty years ago. This interest is mingled with philanthropy, and is apt to be a little didactic in the expression of its regard. Wilkie Collins, indeed, after the easy-going fashion of his generation, was content to take the Unknown Public as he found it, and to wonder vaguely whether the same man wrote all the stories that were so fearfully and wonderfully alike: "a combination

of fierce melodrama and meek domestic sentiment; short dialogues and paragraphs on the
French pattern, with English moral reflections
of the sort that occur on the top lines of children's copybooks; descriptions and conversations for the beginning of the number, and a
'strong situation' dragged in by the neck and
shoulders for the end." It was in the Answers to Correspondents, however, that the distinguished novelist confesses he took the keenest delight, — in the punctilious reader, who
is anxious to know the correct hour at which
to visit a newly married couple; in the practical reader, who asks how to make crumpets
and liquid blacking; in the sentimental reader,
who has received presents from a gentleman to
whom she is not engaged, and desires the editor's sanction for the deed; in the timorous
reader, who is afraid of a French invasion and
of dragonflies. The scraps of editorial wisdom
doled out to these benighted beings were, in
Wilkie Collins's opinion, well worth the journal's modest price. He was rejoiced to know
that "a sensible and honorable man never
flirts himself, and ever despises flirts of the
other sex." He was still more pleased to be

told, " When you have a sad trick of blushing, on being introduced to a young lady, and when you want to correct the habit, summon to your aid a serene and manly confidence."

Members of the Known Public who explore the wilds and deeps of penny fiction to-day are less satisfied with what they see, less flippant in their methods of criticism, and less disposed to permit mankind to be amused after its own dull fashion. " Let us raise the tone of these popular journals," is their cry, "and we shall soon have millions of readers taking rational delight in wholesome literature. Let us publish good stories at a penny apiece, — in fact, it is our plain duty to do so, — and these millions of readers will, with grateful hearts, rise up and call us blessed." To which Mr. Payn responds mirthfully that the Unknown Public is every whit as sure of what it wants as the Known Public that aspires to teach it, and perhaps even a little surer. " The Count of Monte Cristo," " The Wandering Jew," " Ivanhoe," and " White Lies " were all offered in turn at a penny apiece, and were in turn rejected. That it does occasionally accept better fiction, if it can get it cheap, we have the

word of Mr. Wright, who claims to have been
for years a member of this mysterious body,
and to have an inner knowledge of what it
likes and dislikes. "The Woman in White,"
"Lady Audley's Secret," and "It is Never
Too Late to Mend" are, he asserts, familiar
names with a certain stratum of the Unknown
Public; "Midshipman Easy" is an old friend,
and "The Pathfinder" and "The Last of the
Mohicans" enjoy a fitful popularity. But its
real favorite, its admitted pride and delight,
is Ouida. The "genteel young ladies of the
counter," and their hard-working sisterhood
of dressmakers and milliners and lodging-
house keepers, all accept Ouida as a literary
oracle. "They quite agree with herself that
she is a woman of genius. They recognize
in her the embodiment of their own inex-
pressible imaginings of aristocratic people and
things. They believe in her Byronic characters, and their Arabian-Nights-like wealth and
power; in her titanic and delightfully wicked
guardsmen; in her erratic or ferocious, but always gorgeous princes, her surpassingly lovely,
but more or less immoral grand dames, and
her wonderful Bohemians of both sexes. They

believe, too, in her sheer 'fine writing.' Its
jingle is pleasant to their senses, even though
they fail to catch its meaning. Ouida's work
is essentially the acme of penny-serial style.
The novelists of the penny prints toil after her
in vain, but they do toil after her. They aim
at the same gorgeousness of effect, though they
lack her powers to produce it, to impress it
vividly upon readers."

It has not been my experience to find in
these weeklies — and I have read many of
them — even a dim reflection of Ouida's mere-
tricious glitter. A gentle and unobtrusive
dullness; a smooth fluency of style, suggestive
of the author's having written several hundreds
of such stories before, and turning them out
with no more intellectual effort than an organ-
grinder uses in turning the crank of his organ;
an air of absolute unreality about the characters, not so much from overdrawing as from
their deadly sameness; conversations of vapid
sprightliness and an atmosphere of oppressive
respectability, — these are the characteristics
of penny fiction, if I may judge from the varied specimens that have fallen into my hands.
The foreign scoundrels and secret poisoners,

the sumptuous wealth and lavish bloodshed,
that thrilled the boyhood of Mr. Wright have,
I greatly fear, been refined out of existence.
There is an occasional promise of this sort of
thing, but never any adequate fulfillment. I
once hoped much from the opening paragraph
of a tale describing the virtuous heroine's
wicked husband in language which seemed to
me full of bright auspices for his future : —

"The speaker was a fair, well-dressed man,
in appearance about three-and-thirty. A yellow mustache increased the languid, *insouciant*
expression of his long, well-cut features, which
were handsome, but, despite their delicacy,
had a singular animal resemblance in them, —
God's image in the possession of a cool, un-
principled fiend, which now and then peered
out of the pale blue eyes, half veiled by the
yellow lashes."

Yet, with all his advantages of physiognomy,
the utmost this pale-eyed person achieves is
to hang around in his wife's way until she
shoots him, — accidentally, of course, — and
secures herself from any further annoyance.

In a taste for aristocracy, however, and a
splendid contempt for trade, and "the city,"

and the objectionable middle classes, our penny
novelist surpasses even Ouida, and approaches
more nearly to that enamored exponent of high
life, Lord Beaconsfield. He will dance his
puppets, as Tony Lumpkin's boon companion
danced his bear, "only to the very genteelest
of tunes." Mr. Edward Salmon, who has
written with amazing seriousness on "What
the Working Classes Read," and who thinks
it a pity "more energy is not exerted in bringing home to the people the inherent attractions
of Shakespeare, Scott, Marryat, Dickens, Lytton, and George Eliot," makes the distinct
assertion that socialism and a hatred of the
fashionable world are fostered by the penny
serials, and by the pictures they draw of a lux-
urious and depraved nobility. "The stories,"
he says gravely, "are utterly contemptible in
literary execution. They thrive on the wicked
baronet, the faithless but handsome peeress,
and find their chief supporters among shopgirls, seamstresses, and domestic servants. It
is hardly surprising that there should exist in
the impressionable minds of the masses an
aversion more or less deep to the upper classes.
If one of their own order, man or woman, ap-

pears in the pages of these unwholesome prints, it is only as a paragon of virtue, who is probably ruined, or at least wronged, by that incarnation of evil, the sensuous aristocrat, standing six feet, with his dark eyes, heavy mustache, pearl-like teeth, and black hair. Throughout the story the keynote struck is high - born scoundrelism. Every social misdemeanor is called in to assist the progress of the slipshod narrative. Crime and love are the essential ingredients, and the influence exercised over the feminine reader, often unenlightened by any close contact with the classes whom the novelist pretends to portray, crystallizes into an irremovable dislike of the upper strata of society." [1]

It is hard, after reading this extract, to believe that Mr. Salmon ever examined any of these " slipshod narratives " for himself, or he would know that the aristocrat of penny fiction is always fair. The stalwart young farmer, the aspiring artist, the sailor lover, may rival each other in dark clustering curls, but the peer, as befits his rank, is monotonously blonde.

[1] *The Nineteenth Century.*

"The dark was dowered with beauty,
    The fair was nobly born.
  In the face of the one was hatred;
    In the face of the other, scorn."

Mr. Hamilton Aïdé probably does not design his graceful verses as illustrations of weekly novelettes, but he understands better than Mr. Salmon the subtle sympathy between birth and coloring.

Neither have I discovered any socialistic tendency in these stories, nor any disposition to exalt the lower orders at the expense of the upper. The Clara Vere de Veres who smiled on me in the course of my researches were all as virtuous as they were beautiful, and their noble lovers were models of chivalry and truth. It was the scheming lawyer, the base-born, self-made man of business, who crept as a serpent into their patrician Eden, and was treated with the contempt and contumely he deserved. In one instance, such an upstart, Mr. John Farlow by name, ventures to urge upon an impoverished landholder his offers of friendship and assistance, and this is the spirit in which his advances are received : —

" The colonel shudders, as he gazes, half wearily, half scornfully, at the shapeless, squat figure of the Caliban-like creature before him. That he, Courtenay St. Leger Walterton, late in command of her Majesty's Lancers, should have to listen respectfully to the hectoring of this low city rascal, while a horsepond awaits without, and a collection of horsewhips hang ready for instant application on the hunting-rack in the hall within! Yet it is so; he is wholly at this man's mercy, and the colonel, like the humblest of mankind, is obliged to succumb to the inevitable."

Now, since I turned the last page of "Ten Thousand a Year," a long, long time ago, I have hardly met with a finer instance of aristocratic feeling than this, or a more crushing disdain for the ignoble creature known as a solicitor. Mr. John Farlow is of course a villain, but Courtenay St. Leger Walterton is not aware of this fact, and neither, in the beginning of the tale, is the reader. What we do know, however, is that, being a " low city rascal," he naturally merits horsewhipping at the hands of a blue-blooded country squire. He would have deserved hanging, had the colonel been a duke, and perhaps that punishment might have been meted triumphantly out to him, for the penny novelist, with all his faults, still "loves his House of Peers."

The task of providing literature for the Unknown Public is not the easy thing it seems to critics like Mr. Wright and Mr. Salmon. The Unknown Public has its literature already, — a literature which enjoys an enormous circulation, and gives absolute satisfaction. One publishing company alone, "for the people," claims that its penny novelettes, issued weekly, reach seven millions of readers, and these seven millions are evidently content with what they receive. Mr. Andrew Lang is responsible for the statement that a story about a mill girl, which was printed in a Glasgow penny journal, so delighted the subscribers that they demanded it should be several times repeated in its columns. "There could not," says Mr. Lang somewhat wistfully, "be a more perfect and gratifying success;" and publishers of ambitious and high-toned periodicals may well be forgiven for envying such a master-stroke. When were they ever asked to reprint a story, however vaunted its perfections, however popular it seemed to be? The heroine of this magic tale is defrauded of her inheritance by

villains who possess sumptuous subterranean
palaces and torture-chambers in "her own romantic town" of Glasgow, the last place in
the world where we should reasonably expect
to find them.    "The one essential feature,"
Mr. Lang observes, "in a truly successful
tale is that there should be an *ingénue*, as pure
as poor, who is debarred by conspiracies from
the enjoyment of a prodigious fortune."    This
is a favorite device with weekly papers at
home, and the serial story, on either side of
the Atlantic, is perforce a little more stirring
in its character than that presented to us in
finished form through the medium of the
penny novelette.    With the first, the "strong
situation" is serviceable as a decoy to lure the
reader into purchasing the following number.
With the second, no such artifice is needed or
employed.    The buyer has his pennyworth already in hand ; and a very good pennyworth
it is, judged by quantity alone.    Wilkie Collins tells us how he tried vainly to extract from
a shopman an opinion as to which was the best
journal to select, and how the shopman persisted, very naturally, in saying that there was
no choice, — one was every bit as long as

another. "Well, you see some likes one, and some the next. Take 'em all the year around, and there ain't a pin, as I knows of, to choose between them. There's just about as much in one as there is in its neighbor. All good penn'orths. Bless my soul! Just take 'em up and look for yourself! All good penn'orths, choose where you like."

Exactly as if they were shrimps or periwinkles! Very good measure, if you chance to like the stuff! "Dorothy, a Home Journal for Ladies," in a rather attractive pale green cover, gives you every week a complete story, nearly half the length of an average English novel, and fairly well illustrated with full-page cuts. Each number contains, in addition, Dorothy's Letter-Box, where all reasonable questions are answered, and Dorothy's Drawing-Room, with items of fashionable news, — the whereabouts of the Queen, and the interesting fact that "the Duke and Duchess of Portland have been living quietly and giving no parties at Langwell, the Duke being desirous of affording the Duchess every chance of better regaining her health." Also Hints for Practical Dressmaking, by "Busy Bee;"

Our Homes, by "Lady Bird;" an occasional poem; and Notes on Handwriting, where you may learn that you have "ambition, an ardent, tender, affectionate, and sensitive nature, easily impressed, and inclined to jealousy.    There is also some sense of beauty, vivid fancy, and sequence of ideas."    Now and then a doubting maid sends a scrap of her lover's penmanship to be deciphered, and receives the following gentle encouragement : —

"LOVE LIES BLEEDING. — I hardly like to say whether the writer of the morsel you inclose would make a good husband ; but I should imagine him as thoughtful for others, romantic and loving, very orderly in his habits, and fairly well educated ; rather hot-tempered, but forgives and forgets quickly."

All this for a penny, — two cents of American money !    No wonder "Dorothy" reaches her millions of readers.    No wonder the little green books lie in great heaps on the counters of every railway station in England.    She is, perhaps, the most high-toned of such weekly issues ; but "The Princess," in a bright blue cover, follows closely in her wake, with a complete story, illustrated, and Boudoir Gossip about Prince George of Wales, and Mrs. Mackay, and the Earl and Countess of Jersey. " Bow Bells " and " The Wide World Novelettes " are on a distinctly lower scale : the fiction more sensational, the cuts coarser, and the pink cover of " Bow Bells " flaunting and vulgar. " A Magazine of Short Stories " aims at being lively and vivacious in the style of Rhoda Broughton, and gives a good pennyworth of tales, verses, Answers to Correspondents, and a column of Familiar Quotations Verified that alone is worth the money. But the final triumph of quantity over quality, of matter over mind, is in the " Book for All," published weekly at the price of one penny, and containing five separate departments, for women, girls, men, boys, and children. Each of these departments has a short illustrated story, poetry, anecdotes, puzzles, confidential talks with the editor, advice on every subject, and information of every description. Here you can learn " how to preserve your beauty" and how to make " royal Battenberg " lace, how to run a Texas ranch and how to go into mourning for your mother, how to cure stammering and how · to rid a dog of fleas. Here you may acquire knowledge upon the most varied topics, from lung diseases in animals to Catherine of Russia's watch, from the aborigines of Australia to scientific notes on the Lithuanian language. The Unknown Public must indeed be athirst for knowledge, if it can absorb such quantities week after week with unabated zeal ; and, from the Answers to Correspondents, we are led to suppose it is ever eager for more. One inquiring mind is comforted by the assurance that " narrative monophone will appear in its turn," and an ambitious but elderly reader is gently warned that " a person aged fifty might learn to play on the guitar, and perhaps be able to sing ; but the chances are that, in both instances, the performance will not be likely to captivate those who are compelled to listen to it." On the whole, after an exhaustive study of penny weeklies, I should say that, were I expected to provide a large family with reading matter and encyclopædic information at the modest rate of one dollar and four cents a year, the " Book for All " would be the journal of my choice.

It is not in penny fiction alone, however, that the railway book-stalls do a thriving trade.

The shilling novels stand in goodly rows, inviting you to a purchase you are sure afterwards to regret. The average shilling novel in England differs from the average penny novel in size only; and, judged by measurement, the sole standard it is possible to apply, it should, to warrant its price, be about six times the length. "Lord Elwyn's Daughter" and "The Nun's Curse," at a shilling each, bear such a strong family resemblance to their penny cousins, "Golden Chains" and "Her Bitter Burden," that it needs their outward dress to distinguish them; and "Haunted" and "The Man who Vanished" carry their finest thrills in their title. Quite early in my search, I noticed at the Waterloo station three shilling novels, — "Weaker than Woman," "Lady Hutton's Ward," and "Diana's Discipline," all advertised conspicuously as being by the author of "Dora Thorne." Feeling that my ignorance of Dora Thorne herself was a matter for regret and enlightenment, I asked for her at once, to be told she was not in stock, but I might, if I liked, have "Lady Gwendolen's Dream," by the same writer. I declined "Lady Gwendolen," and at the next station once more demanded "Dora Thorne." In vain! The young man in attendance glanced over his volumes, shook his head, and offered me "Diana's Discipline," and a fresh book "The Fatal Lilies," also by the author of "Dora Thorne." Another stall at another station had all five of these novels, and a sixth one in addition, "A Golden Heart," by the author of "Dora Thorne," but still no "Dora." Elsewhere I encountered "Her Martyrdom" and "Which Loved Him Best," both stamped with the cabalistic words "By the Author of 'Dora Thorne';" and so it continued to the end. New stories without number, all from the same pen, and all countersigned "By the Author of 'Dora Thorne,'" but never "Dora." From first to last, she remained elusive, invisible, unattainable, — a Mrs. Harris among books, a name and nothing more.

Comedy is very popular at railway bookstalls: "My Churchwardens," by a Vicar, and "My Rectors," by a Quondam Curate; a weekly pennyworth of mild jokes called "Pick-Me-Up," and a still cheaper and still milder collection for a half-penny called "Funny Cuts;" an occasional shabby copy of "Inno-

cents Abroad," which stands as the representative of American humor, and that most mysterious of journals, "Ally Sloper's Half Holiday,"
which always conveys the impression of being
exceedingly amusing if one could only understand the fun. Everybody — I mean, of
course, everybody who rides in third-class car-
riages — buys this paper, and studies it so-
berly, industriously, almost sadly; but I have
never yet seen anybody laugh over it. Mrs.
Pennell, indeed, with a most heroic devotion
to the cause of humor, and a catholic appreciation of its highways and byways, has analyzed
Ally Sloper for the benefit of the Known
Public which reads the "Contemporary Review," and claims that he is a modern brother
of old-time jesters, — of Pierrot, and Pulci-
nello, and Pantaleone; reflecting national
vices and follies with caustic but good-natured
fidelity. " While the cultured of the present
generation have been busy proving their powers of imitation," says Mrs. Pennell, "this
unconscious evolution of a popular type has
established the pretensions of the people to
originality." But, alas! it is not given to the
moderately cultivated to understand such types

without a good deal of interpretation; and merely buying and reading the paper are of very little service. Here are the pictures, which I am told are clever; here is the text, which is probably clever, too; but their combined brilliancy conveys no light to my mind. Ally Sloper leading "a local German band" at Tenby, Ally Sloper interviewing distinguished people, may, like Mr. F.'s aunt, be "ingenious and even subtle," but the key to his subtlety is lacking. As for Tootsie, and The Dook Snook, and Lord Bob, and The Hon. Billy, and all the other members of this interesting family who play their weekly part in the recurring comedy, they would be quite as amusing to the uninitiated reader if they followed the example of the erudite Oxonian, and conversed in "the Ostiak dialect of Tungusian."

By way of contrast, I suppose, the other comic weeklies preserve a simplicity of character which is equaled only by their placid and soothing dullness. It is easy to understand the amount of humor conveyed in such jests as these, both of which are deemed worthy of half-page illustrations.

"*Aunt Kate* (in the park). Tell me, Ethel, when any of the men look at me.

" *Little Ethel.* It's me they look at, aunty. You're too old."

" Dear friends again. *Madge* (rather elderly). What do you think of my new hat, Lily?

" *Lily.* It's rather old-fashioned, dear, but it suits you."

This is the very meekest of funning, and feminine tartness and juvenile precocity must be at a low ebb with the Unknown Public when it can relish such shadowy thrusts, even at increasing years, which, from the days of the prophet to the days of Mr. Gladstone, have ever been esteemed a fitting subject for mirth. The distance between the penny dreadful and " Lorna Doone " is not vaster than the distance between these hopeless jests and the fine cynicism, the arrowy humor, of Du Maurier. Mrs. Pennell says very truely that Cimabue Brown and Mrs. Ponsonby de Tomkyns would have no meaning whatever for the British workman, — would probably be as great a mystery to him as The Dook Snook and The Hon. Billy are to me. But Punch's dear little lad who, on a holiday afternoon, has caught only one fish, " and that was so young it did n't

know how to hold on," and the charitable but
near-sighted old lady who drops a penny into
the hat of a meditative peer, come within the
scope of everybody's comprehension.  If more
energy is to be exerted " in bringing home to
the people the inherent attractions of Shakespeare, Scott, Marryat, Dickens, Lytton, and
George Eliot," according to the comprehensive
programme laid out by Mr. Salmon, why not,
as a first step, bring home to them the attractions of a bright, clean, merry jest ?  It might
enable them, perhaps, to recognize the gap
between the humor of George Eliot and the
humor of Captain Marryat, and would serve
to prick their dormant critical faculties into
life.

The one sad sight at an English railway
book-stall is the little array of solid writers
who stand neglected, shabby, and apart, plead-
ing dumbly out of their dusty shame for recognition and release.   I have seen Baxter's
"Saint's Rest" jostled contemptuously into a
corner.   I have seen "The Apostolic Fathers"
hanging their hoary heads with dignified humility, and "The Popes of Rome" lingering
in inglorious bondage.   I have seen our own

Emerson broken-backed and spiritless; and, harder still, "The Autocrat of the Breakfast-Table" shorn of his gay supremacy, frayed, and worn, and exiled from his friends. I have seen "Sartor Resartus" skulking on a dark shelf with a yellow-covered neighbor more gaudy than respectable, and I have seen Buckle's boasted "Civilization" in a condition that would have disgraced a savage. These Titans, discrowned and discredited, these captives, honorable in their rags, stirred my heart with sympathy and compassion. I wanted to gather them up and carry them away to respectability, and the long-forgotten shelter of library walls. But light-weight luggage precluded philanthropy, and, steeling my reluctant soul, I left them to their fate. Still they stand, I know, unsought, neglected, scorned, while thousands of "Dorothys" and "Ally Slopers" are daily sold around them. "How had the star of this daughter of Gomer waxed, while the star of these Cymry, his sons, had waned!" How shall genius be revered and honored, when buried without decent rites in the bleak graveyard of a railway book-stall?

www.ingramcontent.com/pod-product-compliance
Lightning Source LLC
Chambersburg PA
CBHW020105030726
47498CB00006B/1961